Acknowledgments

It has been said that no man is an island. This goes doubly for authors. In writing, an author owes much to past, present, and future influences that knowingly or unknowingly contribute to a work.

I have met, communicated with, and drawn inspiration from myriad people who helped *100 Best Denver Area & Front Range Day Hikes* come to fruition. Many are unsung: those of the past who pioneered the trails and set the standard for excellence in maintaining Colorado's superb natural resources, those of the present who influence what is encompassed in the book you hold and why, and those who will someday walk these trails— glad for the guidance and care of those before them, glad of heart and mind. For all this and more, I am deeply grateful.

All those who lifted this book into being, please accept my humble gratitude. Some that come colorfully to mind are: First and foremost, photographer David Irwin, who also happens to be my beloved husband and good hiking companion.

And, with her insights and initial editorial help, Kelly Fitterer, my valiant daughter upon whom I depend to smooth out the rough edges of a raw manuscript.

Further, I am always pleased and proud to be accompanied on trial trails by my ever-ready, best-friend hiking buddies, Jan Richings and Pat Whittall.

And those at Westcliffe Publishers, especially John Fielder, Linda Doyle, Elizabeth Train, Jenna Browning, Angie Lee, and Craig Keyzer, who saw this book through so that readers may come to know the hiking possibilities in the wonderful state of Colorado.

Others whose invaluable input helped this hiking guide come to fruition are: Cody Duffney, Joel Zenzic, Loraine Yeatts, and Laura Hagar who, from the beginning, encouraged me to write nature guides. Thank you all.

For those who use this book to explore the wondrous outdoors, I am grateful you have chosen *100 Best Denver Area & Front Range Day Hikes* as your guide.

Finally, a bowed head to the Creator of all this natural wonder we know as Earth.

Pristine boulder raspberry blossoms match the distant Continental Divide's snowy mantle.

Contents

Wildflowers and gleaming water reward hikers at Loch Lomond's inlet.

Regional Map

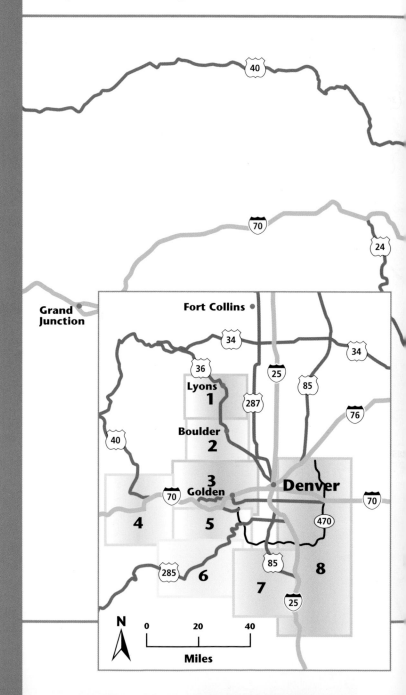

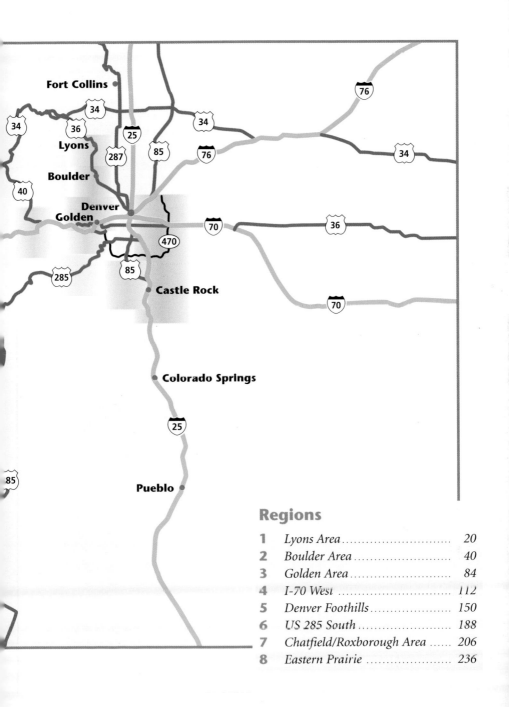

11

Fort Collins

76

34

34

34

36

25

Lyons

287   85   76   34

Boulder

40

Denver
Golden

70   36

470

285   85

Castle Rock

70

Colorado Springs

25

85

Pueblo

Regions

Introduction

Each time I see an eagle, the majesty of freedom soars in my earthbound soul. It began long ago, this eagle thing. From early on I can recall being asked the age-old question, "If you could change into an animal, what would you choose to be?" My answer has always been "an eagle." Soaring ever so high and free above those tethered to the ground, or even most other birds, was my dream. Imagine rising along thermals, spiraling on an eight-foot wingspan, until earthbound creatures could hardly see you—a speck in the sky. But your bright golden eyes, keen as telescopes, could perceive the slightest movements below.

Over the years, many an eagle has soared above me in the blue-bowl sky of Colorado. Their presence enriched my hikes, and left me feeling privileged, having been beneath an eagle's wing. Of all the overhead encounters, however, one stands out as a particularly special moment.

It was a true Colorado tempera-painted day. For the last time before it was officially opened to the public, the main trail loop in Roxborough State Park called my restless feet to task. I soaked in the solitude of being alone on the trail. Upon finishing the loop, I returned to find the visitor center patio nearly hidden under folding chairs and chatting folks, for this was the day that Roxborough was to be dedicated. In addition to enthusiastic naturalists and dignitaries, including the governor, was a small group of Native Americans who had come to bless this park and all it holds.

Solemn Indian dancers moved the onlookers to be as still as the late-spring air. And through that stillness, a thin, purifying plume of burning sage and cedar wound skyward. A dignified tribal member invoked a prayer to the Great Spirit. And as one, all present, compelled by I know not what, lifted our eyes to the sky. A golden eagle soared above our hushed heads, blessing this ceremony and encircling the park with shining bronze feathers and golden eyes.

When I walk the trails in this book, many of which are graced by wide, golden wings, I am humbly reminded of all with whom we share the earth, or perhaps, more appropriately, all who share the earth with us. These trails, each within an hour's drive of Denver, are testaments to the diverse and fulfilling experience of day hiking. City trails cloistered by shade and tucked out of suburban sight, foothill routes that can be reached after work for an evening outing, montane hikes that feel remote, and high-country tundra treks—they're all waiting for your footsteps.

May you walk under wide Colorado skies, and perhaps beneath an eagle's wings.

—*Pamela D. Irwin*

Trekking to Lower Chicago Lake, the author finds interest and majesty everywhere.

How To Use This Guide

Regional Designations and Maps

This book is arranged geographically for ease in locating trails and is color-coded for quick reference. The eight distinct regions outlined in the guide encompass areas that share similar access points, such as towns and main highways. Regional maps introduce each section.

I always recommend stopping at a visitor center, consulting the map at trailhead kiosks, and picking up a trail brochure when these amenities are available. The following maps are good supplementary resources: Trails Illustrated's *Map 100, Boulder/Golden; Front Range Recreation Topo Map* from Latitude 40°. DeLorme's *Colorado Atlas & Gazetteer* is also a helpful source map for getting to and from the hikes in this book.

Of interest in all seasons, the ponds along the Audubon Discovery Loop are waterfowl magnets.

Hike Listings

Each hike description carefully outlines the route, with particular attention given to areas of interest and sections of trail that might cause confusion. Parking availability, weather concerns, and other particulars are mentioned at the beginning of each hike description.

Trail Rating Each of these trails has been hiked—some several times—and rated for the everyday hiker. Hikes rated easy are suitable for hikers of most ages and abilities. Moderate and strenuous designations are given to hikes with rugged terrain, high-elevation trailheads, substantial elevation gain, significant mileage, or a combination of all four factors.

Trail Length Round-trip mileage is given for each route, whether it is an out-and-back or a loop, unless otherwise noted. The hikes in this book range from easy, level saunters of less than a mile to 12-mile treks, with everything in between. Note that a trail with low mileage is not necessarily easy, as elevation and terrain also determine hike difficulty.

Elevation The first figure noted is always the elevation at the trailhead. The second, in cases where only two numbers are listed, is the high or low point of the hike. If there are more than two numbers given, they represent the high and low points of the hike when the trailhead is neither, indicating large ascents and descents in the route.

Amenities The trailheads in this book vary from those with restroom facilities, picnic areas, and visitor centers to mere gravel pullouts on the side of the road. The information in this section gives you an idea of what to expect at the start of your hike so you can plan accordingly.

Highlights These tidbits are provided to give you a sense of the distinctive qualities of each trail. Some trails in this guide are known for seasonal wildflower shows while others are punctuated by spectacular rock formations, historic ruins, or outstanding views.

Location Most of the trails in this guide are under the jurisdiction of County Parks & Open Space, City Parks & Open Space, State Parks, or National Forest. For contact information, see page 252.

Directions Detailed directions to the trailhead, oriented from the nearest major highway or interstate, are provided for each hike.

On the Trail

Trail Terms

Crusher-fines: a trail surface of stone granules used for its superior drainage qualities.

Multi-use trail: a trail that is open to various users including hikers, bikers, and equestrians. Multi-use trails require that all users be alert and courteous to one another. Bikers must yield to all other users, and hikers must yield to equestrians.

Loop: a circuit, often composed of a number of trails, that begins and ends at the same point.

Balloon loop: a loop that is accessed by a short section of out-and-back trail, referred to as the "string."

Keyhole loop: a short loop accessed by a longer section of out-and-back trail, resembling the skeleton keyholes of yore.

Reverse keyhole loop: a hike that begins with a short loop with a long section of out-and-back trail at its farthest point.

Out-and-back: a route characterized by the fact that it goes out and comes back on the same trail.

Social spur or social trail: an unmarked path, often made by careless foot traffic, that is not maintained by the Park or Forest Service. These trails can cause confusion and wrong turns, so be alert!

Wildflowers color the trail on the Hayden/Green Mountain Loop.

Trail Etiquette

It is important to follow the principles of Leave No Trace Outdoor Ethics even if you are only out for a short jaunt.

- Plan ahead and prepare
- Travel on durable surfaces
- Dispose of waste properly
- Leave what you find
- Minimize impact
- Respect wildlife
- Be considerate of other users

For more information on smart trail use, contact LNT at 1-800-332-4100 or www.LNT.org.

On multi-use trails, bikers yield to all other users and hikers yield to equestrians. When a horse and rider approaches you on the trail, step off the trail, downhill from the horse if possible, and let it pass. Always keep pets leashed and under control when passing other trail users.

Stay on the established trail, even when it is wet or muddy, so as not to cause erosion or other damage to the surrounding area. Do not establish or enhance social trails.

On the Trail

Safety Precautions

Water

It is important to bring and drink plenty of water on your hike. DO NOT drink water from rivers, streams, or ponds unless it has been properly treated.

Weather

Weather in the mountains is changeable. Always be prepared for rain and wind even if you begin your hike under a perfect blue sky. The months of July and August are the height of the summer thunderstorm season, and these tempests can be particularly dangerous in the high country. Plan to complete your hike by midday in order to avoid an electrifying experience while on the trail.

Wildlife

Wildlife is just that—wild. Even the cheekiest chipmunks and most charming gray jays should not be the benefactors of your trailside picnic. Your food is not healthy for these creatures, and animals should never be encouraged to depend on human handouts.

If you chance to encounter larger beasts, such as bighorn sheep, deer, or elk, consider yourself fortunate. However, these animals should be given a wide berth, and must always be observed and photographed from a distance.

Sadly, theft has become a problem at many Denver-area trailheads. Never leave valuables—hidden or otherwise—in your car.

Dedication

To David

He was part of my dream. . .but then I was part of his dream, too.

—*Lewis Carroll*
Through the Looking-Glass

And for those who hold nature as part of their dreams. . .

Lyons Area

From level farm- and rangeland saunters to riverside ambles and treks through challenging terrain, plenty of choices for a satisfying day hike fill the area near Lyons, 16 miles north of Boulder on US 36. This region marks the entrance to North and South St. Vrain Canyons and, to the south, Lefthand Canyon—all three replete with diverse trails. The native sandstone in these lovely canyons was used to construct many of the now historic buildings in the Lyons area.

You'll cross territory esteemed by early Native Americans, settled by homesteaders, and protected in the present day through the Boulder County Open Space program—places such as Heil Valley Ranch, Hall Ranch, Pella Crossing, and Rabbit Mountain. Even the drives to the trailheads brim with splendid scenery, allowing you to get a feel for the countryside that supports the trails upon which you might choose to hike.

Ponderosa pines punctuate the trail on the Wapiti/ Ponderosa Loop.

Contents

Lyons Area
Hikes 1 – 8

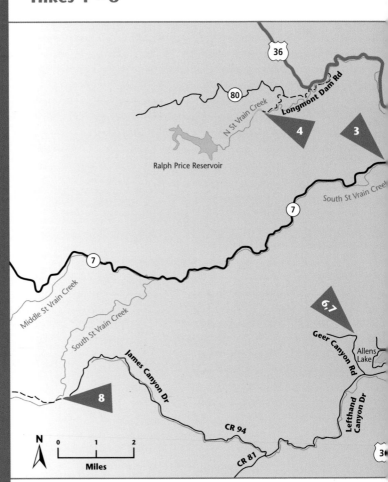

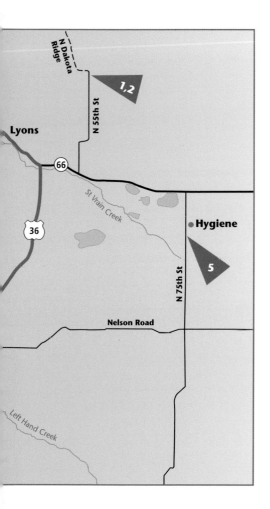

Little Thompson Overlook

Trail Rating	easy to moderate
Trail Length	3-mile out-and-back
Elevation	5,500 to 6,000 feet
Amenities	restrooms, picnic shelter
Highlights	spring wildflowers, overlook
Location	Rabbit Mountain, Boulder County Open Space
Directions	Take US 36 north from Boulder, and turn right onto CO 66 at the "T" intersection. Go approximately 1 mile, turn left on 55th Street, and continue for about 2 miles. Look for parking on the right-hand side of the road.

In spring, the wildflowers on Rabbit Mountain make this Boulder County Parks and Open Space locale a special place. The hike to Little Thompson Overlook offers a quick trek into this nearly 1,400-acre open space. The overlook objective is reached by zigzagging up the 1.5-mile-long trail, the rockiness of which calls for hiking boots, the completion of which calls for celebration.

The designated parking places are prized on fine-weather weekends. Thunderstorms arise quickly on summer afternoons, and this trail is fairly exposed, requiring a degree of weather awareness.

The trailhead kiosk is the place to check the map and begin your trek up to the Little Thompson Overlook. It may be of interest that today's Rabbit Mountain was once known as Rattlesnake Mountain. Early Indians who trod the earth here no doubt respected that reptilian designation.

Imitating resident rattlers, bull snakes, which reside here too, shake their puny tails when alarmed. All snakes deserve a wide berth. Coyotes and deer also call this place home.

The wide sloping hillside, studded by boulders and prickly pear cactus, is traversed by a rocky path that ascends through seasonal wildflowers. Zigzag up and note the plant species that flourish in the disturbed sides of the trail, such as early purple ground cherry.

Following a multi-use sign, the track snakes into the ponderosa pine belt, and a view to the south reveals the Boulder Valley. West of Boulder, the iron-oxide-stained slabs of the Flatirons Formation project into the foothills landscape.

   While the trail grows more rugged underfoot, the gradient eases. You will enter shrubland where an occasional fire-singed pine attests to the fact that landscape can change in a flash. An early season wildflower parade brings hikers up to a trail junction sign indicating that the Little Thompson Overlook is 1 mile to the left. Grass dominates the open land as it spreads across the leveling hillside. Late summer brings sprigs of gayfeather, giving the landscape a rosy-purple cast.

   Before long, a trail sign alerts hikers to the rugged path ahead. Look for ripple-marked slabs, evidence that an inland sea lapped here in the age of dinosaurs. Another junction leads from the rocky passage onto a solid track. In good rain years, a grassy swale at a bend in the trail sports wildflowers such as sunny meadow arnica.

   Follow the contour of a big bluestem-covered hillside, and crest a gentle ridge where the view is to the north. Bump along this rocky track until you arrive at a sign announcing the Little Thompson Overlook, named for the small waterway to the north called the Little Thompson River.

   Obscured as it is by cottonwoods where it emerges from its drainage, the Little Thompson is timid in appearance; but the canyon scenery isn't. Colorful sandstone anticlines form powerful walls that cradle the valley.

   A memorial bench, moored in bedrock, anchors the shrub-surrounded overlook. (Respect the private property beyond.) Views northwest are of mountains, and those to the east are of hogbacks and the Great Plains.

   Wildflowers and wide skies conspire with breathtaking glimpses of geologic past to make this short hike a pleasant jaunt on the rocky swell called Rabbit Mountain.

Eagle Wind Loop

Millennia of hunter-gatherers, the last being the Arapaho, trod Rabbit Mountain. Natural springs, plentiful game, edible plants, wide vistas for security, and the snowy peaks to the west for spirituality, drew nomadic tribes here. Today, you can follow in the footsteps of early native peoples and trek among nearly 1,500 acres of Boulder County Open Space.

Just 15 miles north of Boulder, Rabbit Mountain's Eagle Wind Loop follows a 4.2-mile circuit. The trail zigzags up to a saddle, then climbs to benchland and is fairly easy going. Rattlesnakes make their homes in this area and may be above ground as long as the weather is warm enough. In fact, Rabbit Mountain was once called Rattlesnake Mountain. Parking is in specific slots, so an early arrival is the best time to secure a space. Watch out for summer thunderstorms in the afternoons.

The trail begins a long, steady, upward pull, snaking along in the company of wildflowers such as raspberry-tinted prairie verbena. Peachy copper mallow and purple ground cherry also frequent the trail's disturbed edges. Rocks increase as the track curves up and gains elevation, ascending in zigs and zags before leveling out parallel to a service road. A signed junction indicates Little Thompson River Overlook to the left,

Trail Rating	easy to moderate
Trail Length	4.2-mile balloon loop
Elevation	5,500 to 5,860 feet
Amenities	restrooms, picnic shelter
Highlights	spring wildflowers, overlook
Location	Rabbit Mountain, Boulder County Open Space
Directions	Take US 36 north from Boulder, and turn right onto CO 66 at the "T" intersection. Go about 1 mile, turn left on 55th Street, and continue for approximately 2 miles. Look for parking on the right-hand side of the road.

while Eagle Wind heads right, across the service road. Next, a sign directs Eagle Wind to the right.

Traversing stony ground, the path lifts the hiker toward ponderosa pines and becomes wide enough for side-by-side travel. A west-facing bench presents a lovely panorama of the mighty Continental Divide.

Most of the elevation gain is now behind you, and the leisurely route curves up toward the east. A fork in the trail takes Eagle Wind right. On the west side of the hogback now, the trail grows rockier and heads into ponderosas. Soon a remnant rock wall appears on the right, adding a touch of human impact. Lichened rocks accompany the trail as it wanders among the pines to arrive at a vista of the Boulder Valley and its angled fins of red sandstone strata—the signature Flatirons. Open grasses reveal a cruising section of track headed south. It then bends east and rises slightly to head north.

A sign confirming that Eagle Wind Trail is still underfoot precedes an area where blackened spaces and sentinel snags stand as reminders of the ravages of fire. The next segment travels where both the Rocky Mountains and the Great Plains can be viewed. Gentle contours push the pathway into pines and toward a view looking north.

Head down a rocky service road, where, in the twilight hours, deer may appear. Both mule and white-tailed deer frequent this transition zone where their territories overlap. Soon the loop veers to the right, away from the service road, and traverses grassy parklands. Charcoal skeletons stand stark against the sky, envious of still-living kin in their fourth century of piney life.

Wending over the saddle, the trail resumes on the west side. After crossing the service road, the path provides another spot to view the Continental Divide. The balloon segment of Eagle Wind Trail finishes at the sign with arrows in both directions. A right turn here brings you back to the bench and completes the string section of this trail.

Rabbit Mountain can be a quick jaunt or a leisurely stroll. Hikers enjoy mind-stretching views and pass over the same ground once silently trod by moccasined feet.

Bitterbrush

Long before the white man claimed this land we call Hall Ranch, Cheyenne and Arapaho were watchful residents. Owned by many settlers in the ensuing years, it was not until Boulder County Parks and Open Space made it accessible to the public that it was possible to hike here. Today, you can hike the Bitterbrush Trail, and even loop around the site of the Nelson ranch buildings. The 2 miles covered in this hike description take you through several habitats—from arid shrubland to riparian landscape, and from pasture to pine belt—to a saddle overlook.

The trail gently rises, then increases its ascent via switchbacks along an approximately 8-percent grade until arriving at a saddle anchored by rock outcrops. This is a multi-use trail, though dogs are not permitted in Hall Ranch or other North Foothills Open Space Parks. Parking is adjacent to CO 7, and, although this venue is low in elevation, don't forget the possibility of thunderstorms on summer afternoons.

From the parking area, peruse the map kiosk and pick up a trail brochure that explains many of the features at Hall Ranch, including plants,

Trail Rating	easy to moderate
Trail Length	4-mile out-and-back
Elevation	5,550 to 6,210 feet
Amenities	restrooms
Highlights	red sandstone formations, varied habitats
Location	Hall Ranch, Boulder County Open Space
Directions	Take US 36 north from Boulder, and turn left when US 36 meets CO 66. Turn left again onto CO 7, and continue 1.5 miles to Hall Ranch on the right. No dogs.

geology, wildlife, and history. Before striking out on the trail, go over the text to help get a sense of the place.

Flanked by meadow grasses interspersed with wildflowers, Bitterbrush Trail commences west on an easygoing track. Gently rising, it curves into rolling grassland. Supporting cacti and juniper scrub, an arid sector crosses bedrock washes in view of tilted, red sandstone bluffs. This is ideal habitat for rattlesnakes. Fortunately, the prairie rattler is shy and will usually slither away if given an opportunity. Giving wide berth to these reptiles is best for all.

An old stock-pond dam reveals this open space's ranching past, as do remnants of wooden buildings. Wander up through rocks to reach a sign for the Bitterbrush Trail, and cross an abandoned roadway. Xeric wildflower cousins, hot blue Geyer larkspur and cool white plains larkspur prefer the lower reaches of Bitterbrush Trail. Prickly pear cactus, beautiful when in soft, yellow silky bloom, spend most of the season homely—in a prickly and padded sort of way.

Leveling and then dipping into a drainage, the track greets the ponderosa pine belt and proceeds to a ravine where a secretive seasonal watercourse blushes with wild rose and geranium. The next section undulates between rounded granite boulders and pines. Gaining a roothold in the lithic soil here is the trail's namesake bitterbrush or antelope-brush, a favorite browse of mule deer.

Rising in zigzags, the path comes upon the remains of an old stone wall signaling an easing of the route. Here the trail passes from ponderosa parkland to open pastureland. To celebrate the 2 miles you've hiked, head west to a saddle where a rock outcrop makes a fine place to have a bite to eat and enjoy the view. For those with larger hiking appetites, Bitterbrush continues on to the Nelson Loop for an out-and-back total of 9.3 miles.

With little effort, hikers reap big gains when trekking through Hall Ranch Open Space. Walk through the ranching past and parkland present of Bitterbrush Trail.

Hike 4

Sleepy Lion Loop

Trail Rating	moderate to more difficult
Trail Length	5.5-mile balloon loop
Elevation	5,850 to 6,650 feet
Amenities	restrooms
Highlights	river, wildflowers
Location	Button Rock Preserve, City of Longmont
Directions	Take US 36 north from Boulder to Lyons. Continue 4 miles and turn left on Longmont Dam Road. Proceed 2.8 miles to the Button Rock Trailhead.

Sleepy Lion Loop at Button Rock Preserve is a trail of varied terrain and floral surprises. It is somewhat challenging in places and feels a bit longer than its 5.5 miles might suggest. Nonetheless, the loop, open only to foot traffic, is less used than many trails in the foothills life zone—that, in itself, is gratifying. Under the jurisdiction of the City of Longmont, Button Rock Preserve, west of Lyons, provides a fine place to hike.

The trail begins riverside on a wide roadway, then turns uphill sharply, crosses a flowery tableland, and zigzags rockily down to a drainage before rejoining the roadway back. The trek down by a tributary creek qualifies the "more difficult" designation of the loop due to uneven and, for a short stretch, wet footing. Sturdy boots are suggested.

Popularity makes parking on good-weather weekends a crowded but doable affair. Arrive early to secure a spot and beat summer afternoon thunderstorm activity.

With the rush of North St. Vrain Creek—more like a river here—in your ears, pass a metal gate and stroll down the broad roadway paralleling the water. Stone walls support an old aqueduct as it shoulders its way through a rocky canyon. Rainbow lichens cover a sheer cliff face near the spillway of Longmont Reservoir's serene waters. Sculpted granite outcrops on the left tuck waxflower shrubs into their worn crevices.

Amber stones glisten in the riverbed as you approach the 1-mile mark, at which point this route leaves the road and climbs left or south up a gulch. The sign says it is 2.5 miles to the dam via this loop trail. The sounds of North St. Vrain River fade in the background as a steady pitch takes the trail up to curve around on itself. The track, likely an old wagon road, is supported by stacked stone walls. Ponderosa pines escort the way to rough, crumbling granite harboring antelope-brush or bitterbrush, a favorite of mule deer.

A saddle carries the trail and levels it briefly before pitching up more steeply. Your effort is about to be rewarded as the track bursts from the pines onto a glorious tableland tapestry. Early summer–blooming, ivory Drummond milkvetch teams with hot magenta locoweed for a splendid show.

Forest frames meadow grassland studded by a few pink granite boulders. The route slowly rises to meet ponderosas again. Rocks dominate a ridge of stunted pines and some Douglas firs as the track roughens, dips, and rises again, creating a roller-coaster rock-scape. The muffled growl of rushing water greets the ear. Switchbacks follow the undulating contours of the land, bringing hikers to a vantage point that overlooks the face of the rock dam and the green lake behind it.

Hiker icon posts guide you to iron gates off a once-paved, derelict road that heads downhill. Decomposed granite takes over as the road turns. Since water flows down, and the path follows a creek, descent is a given. Aspen and lush vegetation claim this riparian zone. It's hard to envision a road ever existed over this rockbound descent, which gives way to what can barely be called a trail. Carefully pick your way down beside the lively creek, choosing between wet rocks and unexpected old concrete steps. Footing is slippery.

An insistent roar intensifies as you approach a thundering dam outflow shooting concentrated whitewater like a gargantuan fire hose. From here, 2 miles of level road take you back to your vehicle.

Quite an amazing trek, Sleepy Lion Trail loops through a challenging bit of terrain, highlighted by a spectacular array of wildflowers. Try it in a year when sufficient moisture allows for floral abundance and when other low-elevation Front Range hikes seem too tame.

Pella Crossing Loop

Trail Rating	easy
Trail Length	2.1-mile loop
Elevation	5,100 feet
Amenities	restrooms, picnic shelter
Highlights	a level circuit around rural fishing ponds
Location	Pella Crossing, Boulder County Open Space
Directions	Take US 36 north from Boulder for 5.7 miles. Turn right on Nelson Road, proceed 5.9 miles, and turn left on North 75th Street. Look for Pella Crossing Open Space on the right in 2.2 miles.

Adjacent to the tidy old farming community of Hygiene, Boulder County's Pella Crossing Open Space is a delight. The flat loop leads around a pair of ponds and exposes visitors of all hiking abilities to water birds, riparian vegetation, pastureland, and old-time farmsteads. Popular with anglers, the ponds fit President Herbert Hoover's fishing quote: "Fishing is a chance to wash one's soul in pure air, and with the shimmer of sun on blue water." Hygiene itself deserves a visit; walk or drive down the main street for a step back in time.

The even and flat trail encircles Heron and Sunset Ponds, and passes wilder Webster Pond, on a nice pathway of crusher fines. Parking, shared by anglers and picnickers, is in designated slots, and includes a special area for horse trailers and buses. Summer thunderstorms sometimes roll across the tamed prairie, especially on warm afternoons.

After securing a parking slot, head for the map kiosk, then take a left to go around Sunset Lake clockwise. Along the west shore of the little lake, rustling cottonwood leaves chat up the breeze as crusher fines crunch underfoot. Late season visitors will find water-loving marsh sunflowers growing tall along a grass-flanked irrigation ditch.

The trail traces the edge of the pond, revealing a homestead with a well-loved flower garden, and, in the background, the brick steeple of a country church. Cattails define a corner of the lake where a connector trail leads to Hygiene's crossroads.

The trail now heads east, with the Burlington Northern Railroad tracks on your left, and white-barked cottonwoods and sandbar willow on the right. The dam on Sunset Lake hosts a connector pathway, but the loop continues east to pass along Heron Pond's north shore, which is often populated with ducks and Canada geese. Pastures and barns provide a bucolic backdrop as a bench invites a break. Wild blue flax, in bloom or round seed, grows nearby. This bench makes a good stop for waterfowl observation.

Lake's end turns the loop away from the railroad tracks, and the trail heads south to a grand patriarch of the cottonwoods, gracefully picturesque in his old age. Now heading west, the pathway parallels the south shore of Heron Pond. Lucky folks might spot monarch butterflies—fluttering beauties with black and orange stained-glasslike wings. Milkweed, the monarch caterpillers' food, is plentiful in nearby areas.

With mountains in the blue distance, the loop arrives at Webster Pond. Lush lakeside habitat nurtures marsh sunflowers up to ten feet tall. This smaller body of water is prime wildlife habitat, and also attracts catch-and-release largemouth-bass fisherfolk. Walking between Heron and Webster reveals many plant species, including any number of grasses. Complete the loop by following Webster's outline as the trail exposes a picnic shelter with a pair of lakeside tables.

A peaceful place amidst verdant farmland, Pella Crossing has broad appeal and is especially pretty when tinted by a watercolor sunset. Stroll the easily perambulated loop, and enjoy a trio of sparkling ponds in this special spot of Boulder County Open Space.

Hike 6
Wapiti/Ponderosa Loop

Heil Valley Ranch is one of the newer stars in the Boulder Open Space firmament. Located a few miles north of Boulder, off Lefthand Canyon Drive, it is set in a valley flanked by rolling ponderosa pine parkland and uplifted slopes. Part of the nearly 5,000 acres that comprise North Foothills Open Space, the ranch was privately owned until recently, which kept the land intact. Heil Valley Ranch is home to many kinds of wildlife, including the only elk herd in the Front Range that still migrates between the high country and the plains. The park also offers the short, easy Lichen Loop. To protect wildlife, dogs are not allowed in North Foothills Open Space.

The first 2.5 miles is on the Wapiti (an Indian name for elk) Trail, and forms the string portion of this balloon loop, as it winds up through ponderosa forest. The Ponderosa Loop sector is 2.6 miles and circles a unique tableland, offering a fine overlook view into the Hall Ranch area and across to the mountains beyond. Parking is limited. Be alert for equestrians and mountain bikers, and, on summer afternoons, thunderstorms.

From the northern-most parking spaces under the pines, head for the kiosk displaying trail maps and information at the road's end. Wapiti Trail begins in front of the kiosk and edges up onto an old ranch road. Cruise along the open valley on the road-wide track.

Trail Rating	moderate
Trail Length	7.6-mile balloon loop
Elevation	5,900 to 6,800 feet
Amenities	picnic sites, restrooms
Highlights	views, tableland ecosystems on loop
Location	Heil Valley Ranch, Boulder County Open Space
Directions	Head north out of Boulder on US 36. About 4.8 miles past the junction of US 36 and CO 7, turn left onto Lefthand Canyon Drive. Continue for 0.7 mile, turn right onto Geer Canyon Road, and proceed 1.25 miles to the trailhead. No dogs.

Soon after you pass a sign indicating the rejoining of Lichen Trail, Wapiti Trail veers left off the road and onto single-track. You'll see a prairie dog town. These plump little critters, who vocalize with "barks," like to soak up sun by standing upright, front paws dangling casually. At the first sign of danger, a keen bark sends these black-tailed prairie dogs headlong into their many holes. An interpretive sign offers illustrated details on this interesting community.

A bridge crosses a shrub-choked ravine and the trail winds up among ponderosa pines and wildflowers. Wapiti Trail continues to snake up, reaching high enough to offer a view of the Boulder Valley and the slanted sandstone slabs of the Flatirons.

A sign indicates it is 1 mile to Ponderosa Loop. Broken sandstone leads to a crumbling building among the evergreens. The trail heads north up to a grassy zone, leading to the junction of the Ponderosa Loop; turn left. Along the way in summer, watch for the western tanager in his tropical-bright plumage of red, yellow, and black.

Rock benches invite a pause. The west-headed trail pulls onto a tableland of rock outcroppings, interspersed with stunted pines and wildflowers. Like an apparition in stone, 14,259-foot Longs Peak rises off to the left. This is a great place to enjoy the inviting view, eat a snack, and watch butterflies sip nectar.

Aiming northerly now, the route grows rockier. A half-moon spur takes hikers to benches and a scenic overlook. Steep talus slopes foreground Hall Ranch's striated red sandstone bluffs. In the distance, snow-creased peaks anchor Rocky Mountain National Park. A close-to-nature quality infuses this surprise tableland, inviting the hiker to take a moment to relax and appreciate the diversity of the landscape

Heil Valley Ranch makes a fine destination for those who seek to walk with Mother Nature along a 7.6-mile trail punctuated by an awe-inspiring overlook.

Hike 7

Lichen Loop

Situated in North Foothills Open Space, Heil Valley Ranch is a recent addition to Boulder County's Open Space program. The land has been utilized by prehistoric peoples, homesteaders, ranchers, and farmers, and its quarries are said to have supplied much of the handsome red sandstone for the University of Colorado. Additionally, this area includes important wildlife habitat. Wildlife in North Foothills Open Space is protected by prohibiting dogs.

Short and easy Lichen Trail is a tranquil loop in the transition life zone, where the plains and foothills meet. The low elevation gives early-season hikers a head start on Front Range wildflower bloom-time.

From the pine-sheltered picnic grounds, Lichen Trail gains just 380 feet in elevation and winds down to follow an old road back to the start. The loop begins and ends in grass-cloaked meadows.

Parking is shared by hikers, bikers, and picnickers in designated, pine-shaded slots or in an overflow area. Summer afternoons brew up impressive thunderstorms.

The trailhead for Lichen Loop starts at the north end of the picnic grounds, by a trail map kiosk. The route crosses a sturdy bridge, spanning a tiny seasonal creek, and heads north along a valley slope. Drifting up a gentle hillside through grassy spaces, the track, flanked by a variety of

Trail Rating	easy
Trail Length	1.3-mile loop
Elevation	5,900 to 6,280 feet
Amenities	restrooms, picnic sites
Highlights	low elevation, early spring wildflowers.
Location	Heil Valley Ranch, Boulder County Open Space
Directions	Head north out of Boulder on US 36. About 4.8 miles past the junction of US 36 and CO 7, turn left onto Lefthand Canyon Drive. Continue for 0.7 mile, turn right onto Geer Canyon Road, and proceed for 1.25 miles to the trailhead. No dogs. No bikes.

wildflowers, then curves somewhat to the east. Wild blue flax is most easily spotted in the cool hours before petal drop or on days with dense cloud cover. Great Plains paintbrush, found only at plains elevations, occasionally erupts in pastel fountains.

Traveling close to ponderosas, hikers might try a nose-to-bark sniff to discern the scent of vanilla, most prevalent on warm days. Where grasslands sweep the landscape, projectile-sharp awns of needle-and-thread grass tower over other species.

As the route zigzags up, trailside rocks display multicolored lichens—a symbiotic relationship between algae and fungi. These sedimentary rocks, broken off from the Dakota Hogback formation on the ridge above, stud a grassy meadow. Junipers join pines when the track begins its zig-zagging descent toward a log rail fence. Glimpsed to the west through pine boughs, rockbound Plumely Canyon is habitat for majestic golden eagles.

Pushing out from forest, Lichen Loop leads southwest and meets an old ranch/quarry road. The loop then turns left and heads back down a drainage valley. Young ponderosas gain a roothold on a bank where a vista of forested hills backdrops the stony drainage. Across the way, note man-made slides of small rock—evidence of quarries once supplying sandstone for distinctive local architecture.

Scattered among pasture grasses, bits of petal color brighten the hike. Saunter beside stunted hawthorn along the level roadway. Before you reach the upcoming gate, a path forks back to the trail kiosk, completing Lichen Loop. If you've brought a picnic, shaded tables are available where soughing pines and birdsong may accompany your repast.

Peaceful Lichen Loop favors strolls in the early morning or late afternoon. Nature lovers appreciate the transition between the plains life zone and that of the foothills. Not far north of Boulder, and just south of Lyons, this 1.3-mile trail is ready for your discovery.

Ceran St. Vrain

Trail Rating	easy to moderate
Trail Length	4.2-mile out-and-back
Elevation	8,330 to 7,960 feet
Amenities	restrooms on the access road
Highlights	hiking to water sounds; calypso orchids first half of June
Location	Roosevelt National Forest
Directions	Head north out of Boulder on US 36. About 4.8 miles past the junction of US 36 and CO 7, turn left onto Lefthand Canyon Drive. Take the right fork onto James Canyon Drive (CR 94) proceed roughly 6 miles to the end of the pavement. Turn right, and proceed 0.25 mile to the trailhead.

Named after an accomplished mountain man and trader, who lived in Colorado from 1802 to 1870, the Ceran St. Vrain Trail parallels South St. Vrain Creek. Not far from Boulder, in Roosevelt National Forest, this hike is known for early season calypso orchid displays, and a fast-moving creek. The lively stream provides cooling sound for the 2-mile downhill trek. Conifers provide cooling shade for the uphill return. Gaining about four hundred feet, the hike is not too taxing.

Parking is adequate on weekdays, but on weekends walk-in campers and hikers can fill the space. Be aware that the forest not only muffles footfalls, but it also masks incoming thunderstorms.

South St. Vrain Creek carves its unrelenting way over bedrock at the trailhead, scouring the granitic stone smooth. A handsome sturdy bridge spans the waterway, putting hikers on the shaded north bank near rugged granite outcrops.

Along the next section of trail, deep forest duff, the decaying organic material provided here by Douglas fir and Colorado blue spruce, provides soft footing. River sounds accompany the hiker through a towering evergreen sanctuary. The well-decayed conifer matter nourishes unforgettable calypso or fairy slipper orchids, most likely encountered in early June. The mythical siren Calypso was secretive, and so is her namesake orchid. Picking or digging a calypso destroys the whole plant, nevermore to enthrall seekers of this demure forest delight.

Down to the right, as you overlook the clear creek, check out a little midstream island sporting any number of wildflowers. Back up on the main trail, drift down a lush hillside before the trail gently rises. Moss- and lichen-cloaked boulders precede a stand of lodgepole pine, a species— particularly in dog-hair density—that creates a poverty-stricken understory. It takes a fire to open the cones of these small pines, exposing the seeds initiating germination.

For a brief stint, the track pulls up and away from the creek. Then a steep pitch heads back down toward the fast-moving water, requiring careful footing. Prudent boot placement is the ticket beneath a towering outcrop, where a cantilevered section of trail is supported by a stone wall. A rivulet trickles in from the left. The downward trend is soon reversed by a gentle gradient, ascending a rocky segment followed by an undulating one. A second little seasonal tributary appears near alders' dappling shade, and the track heads into drier habitat.

The trail drops to a shallow ford where an old road crosses, ending the 2-mile trek. Talkative South St. Vrain Creek carries on burbling conversation, unaware of booted eavesdroppers' smiles. This might be a good spot to shed boots and cool tired feet.

For a river-and-forest jaunt not far from Boulder, give amiable and varied Ceran St. Vrain Trail a try. Those on the lookout for exquisite pink calypso orchids should visit in early June.

Boulder Area

Sometimes labeled with such tongue-in-cheek terms as "The People's Republic of Boulder" or "Planet Boulder," this distinctive town is home to more than its share of outdoor enthusiasts who luxuriate in the fact that a plethora of diverse trails are only minutes from their doorsteps. It's only natural that Boulder would be the hiking hub of the northern Front Range.

This glen, at the foot of the Flatirons behind NCAR, hosts a treasure trove of wildflower blooms.

Snuggled up against some of the most prime trails around, this region, roughly 30 miles north of Denver on US 36, claims hikes from flat to somewhat steep, from rolling to rather rugged—and everything in between. The unique Boulder Mountain Park laces the city with open space and maintains urban trails. Boulder County's Walker Ranch and Betasso Open Space Parks lie in this region as well—quick escapes that feel worlds away. Eldorado Canyon State Park sits to the south, serving as a playground for hikers, rock climbers, and mountain bikers, as well as a haven for those seeking stillness and peace a stone's throw from the south end of town. In other words, the Boulder area has something for everyone who loves to explore and experience the out-of-doors.

Contents

Boulder Area

Hikes 9 – 28

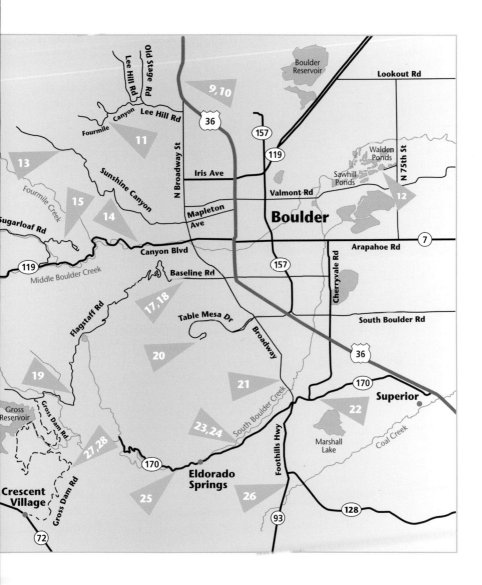

Hogback Ridge Loop

Low elevation, diverse wildflower species, and views grace the Hogback Ridge balloon loop. Cresting at the top of the Dakota Hogback formation, this fine hike supplies a grand view all the way to the white "peaks" of Denver International Airport. Sited just north of the city of Boulder, this Boulder Open Space was once the hunting grounds of the Native Americans who called this area home.

Foothills Trail, forming the string of the balloon, leads to the Hogback Ridge Loop by tunneling under US 36 and curving up a drainage to meet Hogback Ridge Trail. Climbing steadily at first, it then pitches up steeply, assisted by log water bars. Leveling out, the trail exposes a secret valley, then rises again before looping back down. Parking on weekends is scarce, as trailheads for several hike and bike routes share the lot. Thunderstorms might darken summer afternoon skies.

Face west in the parking lot for a view of the Dakota Hogback, the goal of this hike. Bikers and hikers share this portion of the trail, including a pedestrian tunnel.

The meadow on the far side of the underpass is colored with wildflowers, and the trail meanders through. The trail narrows and roughens before coming upon a cattail-screened pond, where a cacophony of chorus frogs sing in springtime. The voice power of male chorus frogs belies the fact that one fits comfortably on a dime. The din will typically stop upon your arrival, but it will resume if you stand patiently silent.

Head through a rusty gate, avoiding patches of glossy three-leaved poison ivy along the way. Take the left fork; the return route of the loop is to the right. Just before an intersection, increasing gradient brings hikers up onto a ravine. Bicyclists go left, whereas the right fork leads west toward ponderosa pines along the described loop.

Trail Rating	easy to moderate
Trail Length	2-mile balloon loop
Elevation	5,550 to 6,400 feet
Amenities	none
Highlights	superb plains vista, secret glen, wildflowers
Location	Boulder Valley Ranch, Boulder Mountain Park
Directions	Head north out of Boulder on US 36. About 0.4 mile past the intersection with North Broadway Street, look for an access road on the right, and follow it 0.2 mile to the fenced Foothills Open Space parking area on the left.

The trail becomes narrow and rough as it pulls up to the junction that begins the balloon section of the hike, limited to foot traffic. (Dogs are prohibited on this section of the trail.) The Hogback Loop heads clockwise or left. Ascending and rocky, then easing for a spell, the trail comes up to a lonely ponderosa. The Flatirons' red sandstone slabs jut into the southern sky, and the I. M. Pei building, housing the National Center for Atmospheric Research, or NCAR, perches on a far knoll.

The incline steepens, assisted by log water bars that create a stairway. Hikers are rewarded at the top with views of the red-roofed University of Colorado campus. The trail heads north now, traveling across a side slope toward ponderosa pines. Some of these trees have been reduced to picturesque snags—casualties of the 1990 Olde Stage Fire.

Guarded by rugged lichen-shrouded outcrops and ravaged pines, the secret glen of Hogback Ridge welcomes hikers to rest. Find a rock in this secluded dell and enjoy a snack while contemplating the works of nature.

Resume the loop and continue upward toward the highest point of the hike. To the west, ranges of forest-cloaked hills create an undulating vista as rock steps lift the trail to a more level stretch. To the right, the very rocky ridge of the hogback might serve as a perch from which to view the eastern plains. You can see clear to DIA's white crown, looking like giant white moths alighting on the prairie, or, perhaps, peaks of snowy meringue.

Begin descending through ponderosa parkland. In spring, lovely wild iris accent this north-facing exposure. The trail zigzags on the way down to a level segment overlooking the Boulder Valley. Dropping again, the loop snakes toward well-placed viewing benches. Cross a seasonal seep on stepping stones for an easy descent, rounding out the balloon portion of the hike. Only the string is left to retrace.

Start off celebrating spring along the Hogback Loop, a quick entry into a world of wildflowers and wide vistas.

Degge/Hidden Valley/ Mesa Reservoir Loop

Wide open spaces and lonely places. Not exactly what one expects to find on the northern edge of bustling Boulder. Nonetheless, this sprawl of space called Boulder Valley Ranch feels deserted, as if only the wind and yucca will be your companions. Loop the Degge, Hidden Valley, and Mesa Reservoir Trails, which form a figure 8 on stark terrain. The landscape is otherworldly—as if you've been transported to a strange and lonesome African savanna—yet cottontail rabbits and prairie dogs seem to be the predominant wildlife. While there are a number of trails in expansive Boulder Valley Ranch, most of them are multi-use. The trails selected for this description are for foot traffic only, and the route gains little elevation in short uphill bursts.

Parking is shared by hikers and bikers, and the lot accesses several trails. The open character here necessitates that summer hikers keep an eye out for afternoon thunderstorms.

From the parking area, go back out to the access road, turn left, and walk up for 0.2 mile along a fence to a signed gap on the right. Head east through a fenced field to quickly reach a sprung gate with Boulder Open Space signage, indicating that bikes are not allowed on Degge Trail. Cross the Silver Lake Ditch and drift down to a view of the Boulder Valley, backdropped by the Flatirons formation.

The track re-crosses the ditch, and heads up a short rocky incline, arriving on a tableland studded with spiky yucca. This useful but no-nonsense plant transforms in June when spires of lilylike flowers shoot up from a roseate of stiff sword-shaped leaves at its base. Descend to a junction with Hidden Valley Trail and hang a right, heading southeast toward another sprung gate. Prairie-dog mounds pock the area. At your arrival, the plump inhabitants will issue warning barks, cadenced by metronome-like tail waggles.

Trail Rating	easy
Trail Length	3.5-mile loop
Elevation	5,480 to 5,530 feet
Amenities	none
Highlights	lonely spaces, view
Location	Boulder Valley Ranch, Boulder Mountain Park
Directions	Head north out of Boulder on US 36. About 0.4 mile past the intersection with North Broadway Street, look for an access road on the right, and follow it 0.2 mile to the Foothills Open Space parking area on the left.

A two-track portion follows, highlighted by sporadically placed wildflowers. In an area of dry disturbed soil, look for ground-hugging silky matted pea's magenta-pink blooms. Curve down onto an easterly heading into a natural drainage where damper earth supports rushes and sedges.

Climb up the far side of the drainage in a northerly direction. As peeled log risers assist your ascent, lots more silky matted pea accompanies your push for the top. Wide skies above wide spaces sometimes remind us that, in this chaotic and crowded world, a wide space of nothingness is of value because of its undemanding nature.

The loop turns left when it intersects with the Mesa Trail. Beyond the berm, the depression that was Mesa Reservoir is lined with struggling trees. Keep an eye out for Colorado's state bird, the lark bunting, feathered in black and white formal wear. This smallish bird might be winging along in dipping flight.

Ending rather abruptly, the tableland sends the route down a short pitch where meadowlarks, dressed in their distinctive, bright yellow bibs, yodel a territorial song. Cruise along a flat section with the foothills rising to the west, and you'll find yourself on Degge Trail again.

Crossing the Silver Lake Ditch bridge leads onto Hidden Valley Trail. Upon reaching the wide dirt road frequented by mountain bikers, step through a gate and cross the road where a lone ponderosa marks a knoll. If you wish, walk a little way down Cobalt Trail to see layered outcrops sporting any number of wildflowers, such as early blooming bladderpod and penstemon. Return to the main trail and travel west inside the fence on the way back to your starting point.

Expansive enough to stretch legs and minds, Boulder Valley Ranch is uniquely appealing. For a cruise just barely north of Boulder, give this many-named loop a try.

Anne U. White Trail

Anne U. White Trail is a pretty, water-accompanied surprise. Practically on Boulder's north doorstep, this pleasant hike leads up Fourmile Canyon alongside Fourmile Canyon Creek. Only 1.75 miles long, the trail, with alternating shade and open space, makes for a satisfying short hike. It is named for local environmentalist and writer Anne Underwood White, who was instrumental in preserving the access land flanking Fourmile Canyon Creek.

Leveling along an old road, then slowly rising on singletrack, the trail's challenge is the nearly two dozen crossings of the little creek. Boots help grip slippery stones strategically placed in the stream. The Anne U. White Trail ends at a boundary sign with private property behind it.

Parking is extremely limited. Try for a hike on a weekday or get to the slots very early in the morning. An early hike may also help avoid summer afternoon thunderstorms.

Granitic slopes, studded with ponderosa pine, greet the hiker at the trailhead. Respecting the adjoining private property, proceed to the information kiosk and pick up a brochure about Anne U. White Trail. A decomposed granite trailbed makes for good walking even after a rain.

Head west into snug Fourmile Canyon until you come close to the creek, where the trail runs by plush patches of wild raspberry guarded by poison ivy. Taking tenacious roothold here and there, poison ivy's characteristic three-part glossy leaves are evident, emerging bronze before turning green. Heed the saying… leaves of three, leave them be. Some of the healthiest poison ivy in the Front Range calls Fourmile Canyon home.

On the right, note huge outcrops splotched with gray, green, and orange lichens. Lichen is a partnership of algae and fungus that slowly breaks down the rock on which it lives. Delicate ferns flourish in the mossy north exposure across the creek. Follow the waterway, burbling in its tawny bed, and notice multi-trunked

Trail Rating	easy
Trail Length	3.5-mile out-and-back
Elevation	6,040 to 6,540 feet
Amenities	none
Highlights	wildflowers, seasonal creek
Location	Fourmile Canyon Creek, Boulder County Open Space
Directions	From North Broadway (CO 7) in Boulder, turn left onto Lee Hill Road (just south of the intersection with US 36). Continue for 2 miles to Wagon Wheel Gap Road. Turn left and continue 1 mile to Pinto Drive. Turn left and proceed to the trailhead and limited parking area. No bikes.

Rocky Mountain maple. Nearby, tiger swallowtail butterflies flit, and tiny blue melissa butterflies, sometimes called blue skippers, "puddle" for moisture and minerals.

The roadway parallels the stream to a great mossy outcrop, where, in May, hikers can inhale the spring-in-the-country scent of feral apple trees in bloom. As the trail curves along this flat segment on gravely soil, the tenacity of ponderosa pine is evident. The huge, bark-covered roots of one such tree crawl fully exposed down broken granite. A stand of quaking aspens makes a lower-than-typical elevation appearance. Soon, gargoyle-topped outcrops appear, bearded in bright orange lichen.

Well-placed stepping-stones simplify a creek crossing, one of perhaps two dozen along the way. Traverse a grassy hillside before dropping back to creek level and another crossing. The stream, looking like gleaming liquid silver, stair-steps down. The trail leads the hiker up through a xeric habitat to a sandstone bench.

Evergreen shade accompanies the next few stream crossings. Like a towering piece of Easter Island statuary, an outcrop on the left supports a slanted sheet of moss. A brief rise of the track brings on drier conditions with more creek crossings ahead.

An outcrop, festooned with a wildflower garden, signals a brief climb up onto open benchland. A seasonal tributary flows down to double the volume of Fourmile Canyon Creek. Follow the canal-like left fork to more crossings and great clumps of dark red–barked river birch. Aspen lead the hiker toward a small fall flowing over smooth bedrock. Use caution where the trail mounts the waterfall lip on the right. Cross the creek for the umpteenth (and last) time.

The water crossings on the latter half of this hike make for fun challenges on shady Anne U. White Trail. Butterflies, birdsong, creek sounds, and wildflowers make this friendly hike on the fringes of Boulder a satisfying outing.

Sawhill Ponds Loop

Trail Rating	easy
Trail Length	2-mile loop
Elevation	5,150 feet
Amenities	picnic tables, benches, restrooms
Highlights	bass fishing, birds, Indian Peaks views
Location	Sawhill Ponds Wildlife Preserve, Boulder County Open Space
Directions	From the intersection of 28th Avenue (US 36) and Arapahoe Road (CO 7) in central Boulder, head east on Arapahoe Road. Turn left onto North 75th Street, pass Valmont Road, and take another left immediately after the railroad tracks at a small sign for Sawhill Ponds Wildlife Preserve.

A gravel extraction pit decades ago, this series of ponds is now a pleasant place for level walking and birdlife observation. Spring is a good time to visit as the area is on a migratory flyway. If you visit at the end of April or beginning of May, courting frogs serenade prospective mates. You might also see golden puffballs waddling along beside their dignified Canada goose parents. Big blue herons and egrets are often seen, as is the blue-arrow flight of the belted kingfisher. Binoculars and a bird book are suggested.

The many ponds in Sawhill Ponds Wildlife Preserve provide an opportunity for anglers to catch both smallmouth and largemouth bass. The large pond at the parking area serves as foreground for a view of the Indian Peaks on the distant Continental Divide. In this scenic setting, a special-use fishing pier juts into the shallow lake. A number of picnic tables, including a covered one, rest nearby.

Built on dikes surrounding the dozen-plus ponds, old roadways serve as trails. The 2-mile circuit follows a flat route that can be quickly hiked for exercise, or strolled at a leisurely pace for wildlife observation.

Parking can be crowded on weekends with fishermen, picnickers, hikers, and birders all vying for vehicle space. While this venue is on Boulder's far-eastern edge and gains no altitude, it still behooves folks to watch for buildup of summer afternoon thunderstorms.

Begin your exploration at the west end of the farthest pond-side parking lot. Companionable in width and inviting conversation, Sawhill Pond Trail sets off along an old roadway. Take a moment at the start to read the posted signs regarding maps and rules.

Pass cottonwoods as you leave the main pond and head west toward a marsh-encircled pond on the left. Red-winged blackbirds call these manmade wetlands home, as do darting dragonflies. A viewing blind on the right is the same one you'll pass later when you complete the Sawhill Ponds Loop.

More ponds at varying stages of maturity appear—some crammed with cattails, others cobbled with rounded stones left from old gravel operations. Along the way, early season hikers may spot dangling yellow tubes of golden currant, scenting the new summer air with the aroma of cloves. Scraggly willow trees are accented here and there by feral apple trees, which provide delightful sights and scents at bloom time.

Optionally, the walk may be extended when you come to a gap in the fence and a sign for Walden Preserve. These Ponds are not as established as those of Sawhill Wildlife Preserve. If you choose not to add 0.75 mile to your loop, continue straight ahead until the roadway turns right, revealing the viewing blind again. Soon, the parking area will appear to the left.

For an easy and companionable saunter, and a good example of natural reclamation and wetland wildlife, Sawhill Ponds Wildlife Preserve is just the place.

Pines to Peak Loop

Just a few miles west of Boulder, up Sunshine Canyon, is a splendid little hike. Pines to Peak Trail loops up and around Bald Mountain for 1 mile. The mountain's igneous dome is not quite bald, but more like the pate of a tonsured monk. Boulder County has given this parkland, where cattle once grazed and miners extracted minerals, back to nature and the outdoor enthusiast.

The trail gains 300 feet in elevation as it carries hikers to a bench with views, before winding back down to the parking area. An early hike puts you at an advantage for a parking space and helps beat thunderstorms on summer afternoons.

The Pines to Peak Trail begins among generously spaced picnic tables shaded by big ponderosa pines. Follow the gentle path under the pines and through wildflower-studded grasses. The decomposed granitic material underfoot is 1.7-billion-year-old Boulder Creek grandiorite. The trail rises to the right, where it meets a fork listed as "summit." Stay to the right on Pines to Peak Trail. Shaded by conifers, the gently rising trail prepares to

Trail Rating	easy
Trail Length	1-mile loop
Elevation	6,860 to 7,160 feet
Amenities	restrooms, picnic sites
Highlights	views, wildflowers
Location	Bald Mountain Scenic Area, Boulder County Open Space
Directions	From 28th Avenue in Boulder (US 36), head west on Mapleton Avenue, which becomes Sunshine Canyon Drive. Bald Mountain Open Space is about 5 miles outside of town, and parking is on the left.

enter a stand of young ponderosas. Before you cross an open area, an inviting bench overlooks rolling, forested hills.

The path travels back among bigger pines where a short, well-worn social spur on the right leads to a pile of boulders with a view. Back on the main path, an old orange-barked ponderosa raises its hoary arms like a surprised octopus. Another bench with a view will appear on the right.

The trail then continues around Bald Mountain counterclockwise as the pines thin and cacti stud the open grassland. The path grows steeper and rockier as it heads up toward the summit, passing through a dry stony meadow dotted with a scattered spiny army, including spring-blooming, green-flowered hedgehog cactus.

At just three hundred feet higher than the trailhead, Pines to Peak Trail reaches its uppermost elevation, where a sturdy pine-shaded bench is perfect for taking in the view. Look east to the plains and west to the Continental Divide. Just off the top, amidst short grasses, drought-resistant wildflowers teem.

Travel in the company of ponderosas as the track winds down again. In spring, hikers will pass through a fairy garden of snowy mouse-ear chickweed and starry pastel phlox. Soon, a junction marks the completion of the balloon portion of the loop, leaving just the string to retrace to the parking area.

This vest-pocket open space offers a gratifying wildflower walk along the Pines to Peak Trail. When Rocky Mountain phlox and delicate mouse-ear bloom in late spring or early summer, the hike is particularly special. The views from Bald Mountain are an added bonus. Attractive picnic sites provide a great lunch spot at the end of the hike.

Hike 14

Boulder Creek Path

Creek sounds mimicking racing wind compete with highway noise along this pleasant jaunt above rushing Boulder Creek. Confined in a rocky canyon just west of the city of Boulder, Boulder Creek Path accommodates hikers and bikers along a wide gentle gradient. Stroll or set a fast pace on this wide, popular pathway that is particularly appealing when early morning sun and shade play leapfrog.

The sector described is just far enough out of Boulder to be a natural surface route. (It is paved in town.) The path follows the stream for just over a mile until it reaches a barrier near a bridge, indicating private property.

Parking, shared by foot and fat-tire traffic, is busiest on weekends. Don't forget that afternoon thunderstorms typically come with the onset of the summer "monsoon" season.

Referred to as Point of Rocks, a great granite outcrop on the right aims you toward an arced footbridge that leads over rushing Boulder Creek. This important water source has made its way down from the high country, giving visitors a cool splash of mountain bounty. As you pass cottonwoods, box elders, and, near the water, river birches, an overhead pipeline defines the Silver Lake Ditch. In the vicinity, shrubs such as serviceberry and chokecherry promise food for wildlife.

Trail Rating	easy
Trail Length	2.2-mile out-and-back
Elevation	5,600 to 5,700 feet
Amenities	none
Highlights	hike and bike path adjacent to Boulder Creek
Location	City of Boulder
Directions	From 28th Avenue (US 36) in Boulder, head west on Canyon Boulevard (CO 119). Proceed up the winding canyon road for 1.9 miles. Pullouts for parking are on both sides of the road. Look for the start of the trail at an arced footbridge next to a large rock outcrop on the right.

Another sign apprises visitors of rules applying to the Boulder Canyon Trail. Winding its way around path-side vegetation, wild grape leads to interpretive signs, one of which discusses nearby narrow gauge bridges built in 1882, the stone abutments of which are still firmly anchored. Beware of poison ivy here—leaves of three, leave them be.

Crusher fines pave the road-wide route. The noisily tumbling creek, confronting myriad boulders, tries to outdo the sounds of the highway. Welcome shade precedes a solid granite wall that frames a footbridge over clear Boulder Creek.

A brief concrete segment takes you under the busy highway and soon a sign stipulates that this point is Mile 2 (although, for this description, it is actually mile 1 since our description starts at a different point than the whole of the trail). Douglas firs and ponderosa pines march down a steep slope where violet-green swallows and broad-tailed hummingbirds dart about.

Lush, riparian vegetation lines the trail as it heads up to the Mile 2.25 sign at an old bridge, signaling the end of the hike. It was here that the town of Orodell, site of both a sawmill and a stamp mill (which prepared gold ore for shipping), flourished in the 1870s. It is now interred several yards beneath CO 119. Another parking area anchors this far end of the Boulder Creek Path, which is useful if the hike is done in reverse.

If you wish to linger on the return walk, check out the short spur just before the bridge near the hike's start. This little trail drops briefly to Boulder Creek for a close-up view of the swirling water and dark boulders—artistic timeworn shapes.

While wildly popular with those on feet and those on wheels, this unpaved portion of Boulder Creek Path is worth a visit.

Canyon Loop

Amidst almost 800 acres of rolling ponderosa pine parkland on the north flank of Boulder Canyon, Betasso Preserve offers the 3.2-mile Canyon Loop, a fine hike in the foothills life zone. Begun as a small homestead, the place was expanded by the ranching Betasso family until purchased in 1976 by Boulder County. The preserve sits atop 1.7-billion-year-old grandiorite, famed for rich mineral deposits. The loop heads down, then gradually up to join an old road before curving back down to a picnic area at the West Trailhead. Head east to complete the circuit.

At the East Trailhead, parking spaces are shared with picnickers. Early arrivals get choice spaces and avoid rambunctious afternoon thunderstorms. It also behooves the hiker to keep a sharp eye and ear out for mountain bikers, who are required to ride the Canyon Loop in a designated direction (which changes periodically). In accordance with present regulations, biking is prohibited on Wednesdays and Saturdays, making them prime hiking days. Begin north from the trail kiosk along a declining slope; the eye is drawn east to a collection of red roofs—the University of Colorado. Drift down a pine-flanked path of decomposed Boulder Creek grandiorite.

In early May, pink spring beauties pop up in the sheltering shade of the evergreens. Pink stars of Rocky Mountain phlox are strewn here in late May

Trail Rating	easy to moderate
Trail Length	3.2-mile loop
Elevation	6,000 to 6,600 feet
Amenities	restrooms, picnic areas
Highlights	a diverse loop over 1.7-billion-year-old rock, views
Location	Betasso Preserve, Boulder County Open Space
Directions	From 28th Avenue (US 36) in Boulder, head west on Canyon Boulevard (CO 119). Proceed up the winding canyon road and make a sharp right onto Sugarloaf Road (5.3 miles from the intersection of Broadway and CO 119). Go 1 mile, turn right, and follow signs to Betasso Preserve's East Trailhead.

and early June. Area fauna include the Abert squirrel, identified by its black coat and ear tufts. The Abert's specific habitat, conveniently providing room and board, is the ponderosa pine parkland through which you now hike.

As the granite-pebbled track levels, you'll cross a service road. A short spur leads to a sturdy bench with a view of the CU Campus. Continue heading west on the main trail. At a seasonal trickle, begin a slight gradient increase. Shallow draws host chokecherry and wild plum whose ripe fruit are sought by wildlife. Other ravines may have seasonal creeks that provide water for the growth of Rocky Mountain maple, river birch, and quaking aspen.

The trail now follows a dry, grassy, south-facing slope, boasting colonies of big bluestem. Ponderosa pine music may be heard when breezes sigh through the long needles.

The route weaves with the mountain's contours high above Fourmile Canyon. Ascend gently now until the path arrives at a switchback. "Undulating" best describes the next segment, as a hillside meadow expands across the landscape and gives it a flowery persona. A viewing bench bids you to relax before the trail heads left on an old roadway. As you travel down the abandoned road, a weary log cabin appears below to the left. Rise steadily to a crest, and follow the ridge to where a sign indicates that Canyon Loop is still underfoot.

Proceed to the west picnic area and restrooms. The shaded picnic tables here may entice you to pack a lunch to enjoy after your hike. Many of the tables sit next to grassy spaces, so kids of all ages can romp nearby. Views of Sugarloaf Mountain, once a prime lookout used by Indian tribes, grace the sky to the northwest.

Not far from Boulder, the convenient Canyon Loop at Betasso Preserve is a hike that feels far from the urban hustle and bustle. A leisurely pace will leave the hiker satisfied and with a sense of accomplishment.

Note: On bike days, hikers may wish to trek in the opposite direction of the bicycle traffic, which might mean following this trail description in reverse.

Sugarloaf Mountain

Trail Rating moderate but rough

Trail Length 2-mile out-and-back

Elevation 8,440 to 8,917 feet

Amenities none

Highlights 360-degree view from plains to peaks

Location Sugarloaf Mountain, Boulder County Open Space

Directions From 28th Avenue (US 36) in Boulder, head west on Canyon Boulevard (CO 119). Proceed 5.3 miles up the winding canyon road and make a sharp right onto Sugarloaf Road. After about 5 miles, turn right onto Sugarloaf Mountain Road, and continue for 0.8 mile to the trailhead.

The famed Switzerland Trail Railroad serviced the area near Sugarloaf Mountain where tungsten mines dotted the rocky hillsides. In 1862, during the Civil War, Sugarloaf Community was established. Today's top values are the views. Boulder Open Space has made the best view of all available to hikers who trek to Sugarloaf's 8,917-foot peak. From the summit, a 360-degree panorama includes a goodly chunk of Colorado mountain-to-plains real estate. The Arapaho sent signals from this flat-topped peak.

A steady 1-mile ascent demands attention on the old cobbled roadbed that serves as trail. Hiking boots are highly recommended. The Sugarloaf Mountain Trail winds up 500 vertical feet until it reaches the flush summit.

Parking is catch-as-can in a casual area. On summer afternoons, it's typical for thunderstorms to brew. Be especially alert to weather on this exposed summit.

A gated road angling up from the eastern end of the parking lot leads to Sugarloaf Mountain. The ascent, aerobic in nature, leads through conifers, and wildflowers sprinkled here and there add touches of color along the rocky way. A fork in the road, defined by a limber pine, can be hiked either way; the right fork is a tad less steep.

As the slant increases so do the cobbles underfoot, so pick your route carefully. Peaks begin to appear as the trail angles up along the southwest slope, including those of the Continental Divide.

Aspens surround the trail where the Olde Stage Burn of 1990 ravaged the landscape. These limber youthful trees embody the continuing healing process. Walking through burned areas reminds us that landscapes can drastically change in no time at all—at any time.

The roadbed becomes very rocky, requiring eyes to the earth rather than to the unfolding scenery ahead. Proceed steadily around the south flank to reach a jumble of angled tumbled granite. The rock-fall flows down the slope until it runs out at a line of chokecherry and boulder raspberry, circumscribed by grasslands.

Curve up, passing a pair of young ponderosa pines, to traverse the east face of Sugarloaf, where flames licked pine patriarchs into blackened snags. Continue across the north flank as the view widens until you reach the last coil, sending you left up a tread as stony as a dry creek bed.

Surprising in scope for just a mile's effort, Sugarloaf Mountain's 8,917-foot summit exults in its 360-degree panorama. Facing east reveals the Boulder Valley and, beyond it, the Great Plains stretch to where the sun rises. Legions of evergreens march north to skirt the crests of Rocky Mountain National Park, highlighted by 14,259-foot Longs Peak. The Indian Peaks spear the northwestern sky, bearing tattered white feathers on their shoulders. The lofty Continental Divide unfolds to the southwest.

Mountainscapes aside, take a moment to pause and enjoy the flutterings of butterflies that sip nectar from Sugarloaf's late spring wildflowers. Watch them land, tasting nectar with sensors in their feet before settling down to sup on their chosen blossom.

Quite a heady place, the summit of Sugarloaf Mountain is indeed a great close-in destination that offers a view far more grand than one would expect at this modest elevation. Put it high on your list of local hikes.

McClintock/Enchanted Mesa Loop

Most of the McClintock/Enchanted Mesa circle feels like a foray through genteel backcountry. The trailhead is adjacent to the historic Chautauqua auditorium, which, along with its old-time dining hall and charming retreat cabins, is still in use today.

The McClintock portion of trail prohibits dogs and covers 0.7 mile while ascending 335 feet. The Enchanted Mesa sector is 1.2 miles. The main Mesa Trail connects the two and adds another 0.2 mile and 110 feet in elevation gain. The descent back to the trailhead is on a wide gentle roadway.

While popular all year, the trails emanating from Chautauqua Park are especially well-used in summer, making parking a bit tricky. McClintock/ Enchanted Mesa parking gets filled fast, but strolling from wherever you park within Chautauqua's quaint grounds is a step back in time. Don't forget to scan the skies for summer thunderstorms in the afternoon.

Trail Rating	easy
Trail Length	2.1-mile loop
Elevation	5,850 to 6,250 feet
Amenities	restrooms at the nearby Ranger Cottage
Highlights	historic area, walk in the woods, Flatiron views
Location	Boulder Mountain Park
Directions	Take Baseline Road west from US 36 in south Boulder. Turn left at the Historic District sign. At the end of the road, you'll see the Chautauqua auditorium and parking at the picnic shelter or garden square.

The McClintock Trail, designated by a signpost down on the left, starts southeast of the picnic shelter. The trail dips immediately into a welter of wild plum, where, in spring, orange oriental poppies greet hikers, followed later by riotous masses of wild sweet peas. You'll track along a tight drainage, where a little creek flows under crowded shade trees. Then the trail ascends and passes to the left of a stone bridge. Persevering along this incline takes you to an open spot for a view of the red sandstone fins that make up the jutting Flatirons. Part of the Fountain Formation, these slabs attract rock climbers. One of the ancient slabs is incised with a gigantic CU for Boulder's University of Colorado.

A set of risers takes you past a steep spur trail. Continue straight ahead on McClintock through populous stands of ponderosa pine. The west-heading trail levels, and its northern exposure nurtures Douglas firs and pines. These conifers, in concert with a deciduous shrub-filled drainage below, make fine habitat for singing birds. Wildflowers spangle open grassy areas.

Log risers lift the path for a meeting with Mesa Trail, and the loop takes a left. Social spurs occasionally veer off, but you should stick to the broad Mesa Trail for this hike. Undulating while rising slightly, the pathway reaches a post that marks Enchanted Mesa Trail. Take a left on the gravel roadway. Wide enough for companionable conversation, this trail drifts down through ponderosa parkland. The pines proffer pools of welcome shade on the way to viewing the Boulder Valley.

Continue curving down to a fine view of red-roofed CU to the east; an about-face offers the Flatirons to the west. Pines give way to deciduous trees such as cottonwood and green ash. The Chautauqua auditorium appears, and the route finds the stone bridge passed earlier. Cross it now and saunter down a roadway, passing along the south edge of the old-time resort. You will promptly find yourself back at the hike's beginning.

The McClintock/Enchanted Mesa Loop is pleasant and convenient, and the ambiance of the historic Chautauqua grounds makes this an enjoyable place to explore.

Chautauqua/Bluebell–Baird/ Bluebell Mesa Loop

Trail Rating	easy
Trail Length	1.5-mile loop
Elevation	5,800 to 6,240 feet
Amenities	restrooms near the Rangers Cottage
Highlights	wildflowers, Flatirons views, historic retreat
Location	Boulder Mountain Park
Directions	Take Baseline Road west from US 36 in south Boulder. Parking is on the left, just past 9th Street.

Chautauqua Park, on Boulder's western periphery, is a retreat in a number of ways. Stroll through the historic streets lined with cottages. Visit the old auditorium, quaint dining hall, and small garden park, or peruse the listing of musical events, lectures, and activities offered here.

Chautauqua also hosts several trails leading into Boulder's diverse backyard. This short pretty loop, combining several trails, begins in wild-flower-dotted meadowland backed by the grand red sandstone slabs of the Flatirons. The route then enters forest and saunters down tilted mesa land in the shade of big ponderosa pines.

The parking lot by the Ranger's Cottage fills fast, even on weekdays, and parking on a weekend can be quite challenging. Try to arrive early on a weekday to secure a coveted slot, and in the doing, avoid summer afternoon thunderstorms. Before starting out on Chautuaqua Trail, stop at the Ranger's Cottage, and consult the area map. The westward view from the cottage is lovely, as the impressive Flatirons jut skyward in the background while wildflowers spatter the foreground meadow.

The grade rises easily but steadily through various grasses such as big bluestem. This colonizing prairie native emerges bluish, turning salmon with the onset of autumn. Wild roses perfume the air in early summer, while perennial sweetpeas perk up midsummer, usually in time to celebrate the Fourth of July.

The broad track, perfect for companionable conversations, reaches a group of rocks where you can look east over the distinctive red roofs and local stone edifices of the University of Colorado. Continuing, the gentle incline takes you past a connector trail to a barrier fence. Shorter grasses initiate entry into the ponderosa pine belt. At this point, most of the elevation gain is behind you.

A wild plum thicket and lush poison ivy patches mark the beginning of a conifer forest sector, where stone stairs followed by log steps lift hikers to a junction. Turn left here on Bluebell–Baird Trail for a brief loop segment. Once you've reached the hike's high point, another junction appears, taking the loop left along Bluebell Mesa Trail.

Ponderosa patriarchs anchor this grassy parkland as you cruise downhill on a slanted mesa. Turn left at the junction at the end of the mesa, and descend to a second junction, where the loop goes right.

Still dropping, the trail passes a nice display of wildflowers and a vista that reaches out over Boulder to the plains beyond. Set your sights clear to the eastern horizon, and imagine Kansas cornfields and acres of sunflowers all facing the rising sun. Traverse a north-facing slope before aiming back to the Ranger Cottage and your vehicle.

Wildflowers and wide views reward the hiker on the Chautauqua/Bluebell–Baird/Bluebell Mesa Loop, conveniently located on the western fringes of Boulder.

Meyers Homestead

Walker Ranch Open Space holds a special gem. A beautiful barn and sawmill building rests in a sweeping, wildflower-filled meadow on the back side of Flagstaff Mountain. The structure dates back to the late 1800s when the property was homesteaded. The building and the parkland that surrounds it is on the National Register of Historic Places as a "historic cultural landscape." The vintage barn is one of many once used to store hay on the Walker Ranch. James Walker first came to the area in 1869, and he and his wife Phoebe operated what was reportedly the largest successful ranch along the Front Range.

The 2.5-mile Meyers Homestead Trail, named for Andrew Meyers, who first homesteaded and logged this land, takes hikers through history. It traverses several habitats such as grassland, riparian, aspen woods, and ponderosa pine, and a colorful array of wildflowers cheers the landscape. The trail curves as it ascends on a moderate gradient, first dipping into a valley, then rising in waves toward its completion.

Trail Rating	easy to moderate
Trail Length	5-mile out-and-back
Elevation	7,350 to 8,050 feet
Amenities	restrooms, picnic sites
Highlights	historic landscape, far-off feel
Location	Walker Ranch, Boulder County Open Space
Directions	From US 36 in south Boulder, take Baseline Road (which becomes Flagstaff Road) west. Continue for approximately 8.5 miles to Walker Ranch's Meyers Homestead Trailhead on the right.

Limited parking is shared by picnickers, mountain bikers, and occasional equestrians, and is busiest on weekends. Try for a weekday morning or evening hike, thereby avoiding the most serious parking competition as well as summer afternoon thunderstorms.

Starting from the Meyers Homestead parking area, Meyers Homestead Trail follows a wide fire road, making for companionable conversation. Dip by a riparian habitat that sports a number of moisture-loving wildflowers such as tall chiming bells and tall coneflower—a cousin of the black-eyed Susans. One of the most vividly intense blue wildflowers, mountain penstemon, favors the exposed lithic soil of the banks cut by the roadway.

Rising, the track passes granitic outcrops on its way to a stand of stunted aspens. Shooting stars, in their bloom season, may grace a small seep by an outcrop. Continue ascending toward more aspens and wildflowers before the trail levels out.

Color-sprinkled meadows stretch north where homesteaders once wrested a living from the land along Meyers Gulch. Their livelihood was primarily livestock grazing, but there is little left to mark such efforts. Curve up around the top of the meadow on a rocky path.

The roadway heads for a ridge dominated by pines with coarse granite underfoot. The trail ends with a somewhat obscured view of Boulder Canyon below. To the west, the Indian Peaks appear. Look north to the bald dome of nearly 9,000-foot Sugarloaf Mountain. In the far distance rises 14,259-foot Longs Peak, the only fourteener in Rocky Mountain National Park.

Walker Ranch offers an easy getaway just above Boulder that's especially fine when a watercolor sunset paints the sky. The isolated Meyers Homestead Trail, with its time-honored barn, provides an adventure steeped in history.

Mesa/NCAR Loop

Trail Rating	moderate
Trail Length	2-mile loop
Elevation	6,160 to 5,800 feet
Amenities	restrooms in NCAR building
Highlights	NCAR, wildflower-filled glen
Location	Boulder Mountain Park
Directions	From US 36 south of Boulder, head west on Table Mesa Drive for 2.4 miles to the NCAR parking lot. The start of the Mesa/NCAR Loop is on the W. O. Roberts Nature Trail.

The Mesa/NCAR Loop boasts lovely views, a hidden valley, and a seasonally splendid array of wildflowers. This loop utilizes portions of the 7-mile Mesa Trail and starts at the National Center for Atmospheric Research (NCAR). The towering NCAR building, designed by famed architect I. M. Pei, is a destination itself. If you're curious about weather, or if you're interested in seeing a roomful of massively impressive Cray Computer components, you should stop in for a visit.

Parking is found in the extensive paved lot east of the NCAR building. To access the trailhead for Mesa/NCAR, begin on the Walter Orr Roberts Nature Trail at the northwest corner of the NCAR building. Look for an engraved boulder honoring Mr. Roberts. Follow the wide crusher-fine pathway, staying left until you reach a sign indicating Mesa Trail is off to the left.

Travel cautiously down rough, rocky tread to cross a slope studded with ponderosa pines. The track bisects a small grove of junipers, the shaggy bark of which, along with sage, provides clean aromatic smoke when burned at American Indian purification ceremonies.

Continue heading straight when the trail reaches a junction. The trail rises along a grassy east-facing slope to steps leading up to a switchback section. Hikers are lifted to the level of an enclosed water tank. After passing the North Mesa Trail junction, the track drops and levels out along a short bypass.

On the left, summer-blooming wild roses perfume a sweet little meadow. The short bypass arrives at an acutely angled interchange where the hiker turns left. The meadow here is chock-full of wildflowers throughout spring and early summer. Not to be missed at peak bloom, great swaths of lupine will astound the senses.

Aiming south now, the trail arrives at the Mesa/NCAR Trail junction, and bears right. After passing through the south end of the dell, the path cruises through stately ponderosa pines. Continue straight ahead, passing the Mallory Cave spur. The footpath levels through conifers. A view materializes through a gap to the east, and the sound of running water soon accompanies the narrowing path as it slants down an east-facing hillside of stunted wild plum and hawthorn thickets.

Upon reaching a wide dirt road, turn left onto Bear Creek Canyon Trail and parallel the stream. A high rock outcrop rears on the left, showcasing a gnarled old pine. Soon after, a post appears on the left and the loop heads left and up. This steep segment begins in a grassy ravine and curls over peeled-log water bars in pursuit of the pine-topped mesa. The mechanical humming of I. M. Pei's soaring architectural statement indicates that you are nearing NCAR and the trail's end.

Right on the edge of south Boulder, the Mesa/NCAR Loop offers a quick hike with good views and great blooming things.

South Boulder Creek West Loop

South Boulder Creek Trail traverses open ranchland on the fringes of sub-urban Boulder, serving as a quick escape from crowded streets. It doesn't take too much imagination to put yourself in a scene from the long-ago, wide-open spaces of "The Wild West." Cattle still graze, cacti still bloom, and a haze of cottonwoods indicates South Boulder Creek's course to the south. Early in the bloom season, wildflowers accent the rangeland.

Parking is in a fenced area adjacent to a small pond, and spots are at a premium on weekends. Don't forget about the possibility of thunderstorms on summer afternoons.

Beyond the restroom, a sprung gate marks the roadway as it heads west past wetlands where pioneers harvested cordgrass to roof their soddies. Jutting spears of red sandstone strata angle into the sky-scape. These 300-million-year-old depositional slabs are from the Fountain Formation, once part of the Ancestral Rocky Mountains. They were named the Flatirons for their resemblance to the irons used by early pioneers.

Trail Rating   easy

Trail Length   4.6-mile loop

Elevation   5,450 to 5,500 feet

Amenities   restrooms, picnic table

Highlights   Flatirons vistas, wide-open spaces

Location   Boulder Mountain Park

Directions   From central Boulder, take Broadway south (it becomes CO 93). Look for Thomas Lane on the right, where a Boulder Open Space sign indicates the South Boulder Creek West Trailhead and parking lot.

South Boulder Creek Trail forks to the right, narrowing as it heads for a copse of cottonwoods. After passing through a metal gate, it resumes its broad path under open skies. With the trail narrowing again as it gently rises, rougher footing leads past old stone walls, probably erected in the late 1800s. The ascent is never taxing as it heads west through sporadic wildflowers.

Upon reaching the Mesa Trail, turn right for a short uphill grade until you come to Big Bluestem Trail. Here the loop takes a right and aims east. Typical foothills shrubs such as three-leaf sumac abound as the somewhat rocky track wends down to cross a drainage. Poison ivy pops up here and there, so beware of leaves of three...

Big bluestem typifies the tall grass prairie that once flourished in these wide-open spaces. This resolute species, also called turkeyfoot for the shape of its seedhead, is a colonizing native grass. It emerges bluish and turns a soft salmon in autumn.

Big Bluestem Trail continues east, widening to road-width from a narrow track as it passes an old corral and barbed wire fences. Cattle may be grazing nearby. Another gate takes you from open space to civilization and Thomas Lane, the last segment of this loop, which leads back to the pond-side parking area.

For a convenient jaunt in an out-of-the-past rangeland atmosphere, try South Boulder Creek West.

Marshall Mesa/ Greenbelt Plateau

Historic Marshall Mesa in southern Boulder County is part of the prized collection of Boulder's Open Space acquisitions. Not only is it beautiful, but it's convenient and enables the hiker to tread in the footsteps of the past. Coal was mined here beginning in the 1860s, and Joseph Marshall erected a blast furnace in order to produce pig iron. Underground coal fires have continued to burn in the area for over 100 years.

Although the area consists of semiarid rolling grasslands today, the vegetation of the Late Cretaceous Period (70–135 million years ago) grew lushly in humid swamps. Accumulated plant matter, under enormous pressure, formed coal seams 12 feet thick. (To create one foot of coal, 15 feet of decaying organic matter is required.)

The trail gently rises, then levels along a community ditch, rises again, and returns as gently as it came. Head-in parking, shared by hikers and bikers, is limited but usually available on weekdays. Watch for thunderstorms on summer afternoons.

From the willow-shaded parking area, head south and climb a few steps past a bridge over canal-sized Community Ditch. The bike path is nearly level as it follows the ditch, constructed in 1885. Marshall Mesa Trail branches off to the left on a narrow path. Where grass once grew horse-belly high, shorter grasses are accented with smatterings of bright wildflowers.

Trail Rating	easy
Trail Length	3-mile out-and-back
Elevation	5,800 to 6,100 feet
Amenities	none
Highlights	views, wildflowers
Location	Boulder Mountain Park
Directions	From central Boulder, take Broadway south (it becomes CO 93). Head east on CO 170/Marshall Drive, and look for the Marshall Mesa Trailhead on the right.

Easing upward, the trail now arrives in the shade of good-size ponderosas. A pale face of smooth stone is covered with historical graffiti. (Just how old does graffiti have to be to be considered historical?) As the path passes a shallow drainage full of ninebark bushes (related to apple trees), a seep wets a smooth sheet of bedrock. The trail opens to a fine mountain view with rolling rangeland in the foreground.

Approaching a gate, the route rejoins the level Community Ditch Trail on the left. Take a moment to enjoy the perfume of wild roses growing along the banks. Beyond a bridge, the path rises toward an old road. Spiky-leaved yucca, a thing of beauty when in lilylike bloom, thrives in the grasslands flanking the route. The creamy blossoms are a favorite food of mule deer.

The track meets the level Greenbelt Plateau Trail on the left. Soon, you'll reach the top of the plateau where great views open. If you are taking photographs, look around the pine parkland for an appropriate foreground to frame the grand panorama of the soaring red Flatirons and sky-piercing Longs Peak.

Marshall Mesa is a fine place to hike—whether for exercise, views, wildflowers, or all three—and can be enjoyed year-round.

Mesa/Big Bluestem/ Towhee Loop

Trail Rating	easy to moderate
Trail Length	3.7-mile loop
Elevation	5,600 to 6,520 feet
Amenities	restrooms, picnic tables
Highlights	wildflowers, Flatirons views
Location	Boulder Mountain Park
Directions	From central Boulder, take Broadway south (it becomes CO 93), and head west on CO 170 (Eldorado Springs Drive). Continue for 1.6 miles to the Mesa Trailhead on the right-hand side of the road.

The southern terminus of the Mesa Trail system lies on the south edge of Boulder Mountain Park. The 3.7-mile loop formed by the South Mesa, Big Bluestem, and Towhee Trails edges the Flatirons' tilted red slabs. Wildflowers and scenery complement each other as hikers pass through the transition zone, which encompasses plains and foothills life zones. The route begins gently, increases in gradient, then gently cruises along a drainage before ascending to its high point.

A large parking area is adequate on weekdays but often fills on nice weekends. Starting out early not only gets you a parking place, but may help you avoid thunderstorms on summer afternoons.

The north side of the parking area is the jumping-off place for South Mesa Trail. After crossing South Boulder Creek on a sizable bridge, head toward a two-story cut-stone building that served as a gristmill in the mid-1800s. The Flatirons dominate the landscape to the west. Their iron-stained sandstone fins, relics of the Ancestral Rockies, thrust skyward.

To the right of the stone house, South Mesa Trail takes off straight ahead through open grasslands studded with rocks, shrubs, and wildflowers. The broad even path rises slowly as boulders appear here and there, and it soon enters a head-high thicket of smooth or scarlet (its fall color) sumac.

About a mile into the loop a sign on the right is marked: Big Bluestem Trail. Follow this access onto an intimate path. When the trail forks, you'll continue on Big Bluestem (named for a tall native grass), head under the power lines, and climb up beside a rocky ravine. The trail levels a bit upon entering the pine belt where views of the Flatirons command attention. Soon an old stone wall anchoring a lovely glade intrigues hikers. Trace the outlines of a pioneer home guarded by a handful of gnarled apple trees.

The trail drops into a small drainage, climbs the west bank, and continues into the shade of a north-facing slope. The reason for the homestead site is just up the trail—a charming little creek. Here, in mid-spring, deep pink western shooting stars may appear. Crossing the creek, the path rises up a few stone steps into an open area of tall bracken fern.

Big Bluestem rejoins the Mesa Trail at the next junction. Turn left, cross a tiny stream, and follow the rising path into the ponderosa pine belt. Stay on Mesa Trail as it curves around a stock tank. Ascending, the companionably wide route traverses rolling pine parkland.

Continue to a posted corner where, just downhill at the next junction, Towhee Trail takes off sharply to the left. This intimate segment, accompanied by the sound of running water, nurtures a secret garden aflutter with butterflies, such as fritillaries and tiger swallowtails. Downstream, a few white-barked quaking aspens grow over a thousand feet below their typical elevation.

Rocky ground drops through dense shrubbery, and the trail meets the little creek a time or two before reaching open grasslands. The end of the loop is getting close, and highway sounds announce the return to reality.

The South Mesa/Big Bluestem/Towhee Loop, southwest of Boulder, offers a convenient escape into the world of wildflowers and diverse habitats—from grasslands to forest to riparian. Birdsong, butterflies, and blooming things highlight this hike.

Mesa/Homestead Loop

With about 30,000 acres of designated open space, the city of Boulder has a big backyard. Running nearly 7 miles along the jutting Flatirons, the Mesa Trail shows hikers a fair bit of these grand grounds. The Mesa Trailhead, at the trail's south end, accesses a network of several loop choices that weave through the area's ravines and canyons. Mesa/Homestead Loop not only offers Flatiron vistas, but has an intimate segment of verdant flowers that last into late summer.

Though the parking area holds a goodly number of vehicles, it is wise to come early, especially on spring and summer weekends. Such a plan allows hikers to enjoy early morning coolness and to avoid the thunderstorms that typically arrive on summer afternoons.

Cottonwood trees and sandbar willow lead the way from the trailhead to a creek crossing, soon followed by a large bridge spanning South Boulder Creek. The two-story stone structure was added to the original homesteader's house in 1874. (The older building is long-gone.) The loop will return to this point.

Heading out, stay straight ahead on road-wide Mesa Trail, and pass through a veritable "forest" of smooth sumac shrubs, which turn bright shades of scarlet in the fall. The rising pathway curves west toward the Flatirons—a 300-million-year-old red sandstone formation.

Ponderosa pines dot the grassy hillside as you bypass Towhee Trail. Continue on the broad Mesa Trail that also passes Big Bluestem Trail after 0.8 mile. The ponderosa pine belt offers occasional shade as you follow the ascending Mesa Trail to a spot with wide views of the eastern plains.

Advancing to a posted intersection under soughing pines, the route takes a left to Shadow Canyon. The forested ravine before you frames a rock formation that could be compared to E.T.'s bulbous-tipped finger.

At this point, a junction sends you sharply

Trail Rating	easy to moderate
Trail Length	2.9-mile loop
Elevation	5,600 to 6,250 feet
Amenities	restrooms, picnic tables
Highlights	1874 stone house, Flatiron views, ferns
Location	Boulder Mountain Park
Directions	From central Boulder, take Broadway south (it becomes CO 93), and head west on CO 170 (Eldorado Springs Drive). Continue for 1.6 miles to the Mesa Trailhead on the right-hand side of the road.

left down a brief segment of the Towhee Trail. Soon another signpost states that heading east will bring you back to the Mesa Trailhead. Follow the trail eastward, enjoying a "secret garden" as you go.

The riparian habitat here, full of ferns, wildflowers, and myriad butter-flies, is the epitome of foothills life-zone verdancy. Even in late summer, after the tall cow parsnip has gone to seed, yellow rays of golden glow and dusty-pink queen of the meadow keep attendant butterflies busy. These graceful insects alight on a blossom, test the nectar with the sensors on their feet, then settle down to sup if the nectar meets their feeding fancy.

Peeled-log steps and stones drop hikers through swatches of minty monarda into a habitat moist enough for quaking aspen—growing well over a thousand feet below their normal elevation. As you proceed down, the canyon mouth opens to a view of Marshall Mesa. Be aware of occasional poison-ivy patches.

A fork in the trail sends the loop right, on Homestead Trail. Cross the creek bed and rise into pines and up onto a tilted, grassy tableland. Descend on a rock-studded track, then drop more seriously down a series of peeled log steps back to the parking area.

Great Flatiron views, fine wildflowers culminating in a "secret garden," and a convenient entry into south Boulder's backyard make Mesa/ Homestead Loop a very lovely hike.

Fowler

Eldorado Canyon's opulence lies in its impressive walls, which rise like wildly painted skyscrapers against the blue Colorado sky. The canyon, fondly referred to as "Eldo" by rock climbers, is famed for its varied and challenging faces and crags. To reach the park entrance, drive slowly through Eldorado Springs. Once renowned for an 1880s Georgian-style hotel featuring a grand artesian spring pool and plush accommodations, Eldorado Springs is a laid-back village today.

Towering rock formations, up to 1.7 billion years old and 850 feet high, flank the impressive canyon. The spectacular entrance once was strung with 7/8 inch cable for a daring tightrope walker who, in his 82nd year, balanced his umpteenth way between the sharp cliffs that characterize Eldorado Canyon. Read about his fearless feats in the fine visitor center at the far end of the road, which provides a good introduction to this unique landscape. Informative brochures are to be found here, including a list called "Birds of Eldorado Canyon State Park."

Visitors to the inner canyon range from serious rock climbers to folks relaxing in the shade of ponderosa pines at streamside picnic sites. It is fascinating to watch intrepid climbers, tiny as firefly lights, navigating vertical faces such as Quartzite, Redgarden, and Rotwand Walls. Wind Tower and

Trail Rating	easy
Trail Length	1-mile out-and-back
Elevation	6,030 to 6,100 feet
Amenities	visitor center, picnic sites
Highlights	impressive scenery, rock climbing or spectating, creek
Location	Eldorado Canyon State Park
Directions	From US 36 or CO 93 south of Boulder, head west on CO 170, which becomes Eldorado Springs Drive. Continue to Eldorado State Park. There is a fee to enter the park.

The Bastille add to climbers' life lists. These ramparts are visible from the gentle Fowler Trail.

Due to Boulder's close proximity, and to the canyon's popularity and configuration, parking is at a premium on weekends. Come early, and don't forget that summer afternoon lightning could influence your visit.

Once parked in a coveted space at Fowler Trailhead, begin hiking from the east end of the parking area along a railroad grade that's never seen a train. Varied shrub species such as Rocky Mountain maple and chokecherry flank the route, as do evergreens such as Douglas fir and ponderosa pine. Wildflowers decorate the edges. Imitating rushing wind, South Boulder Creek sounds off below. Along the way, a sandstone boulder topped with a coiled rattlesnake made of bronze announces interpretive signs explaining the prairie rattler and a rare butterfly: the hops azure.

Narrowing, the trail comes alongside a steep slope of tumbled rock that precedes the junction with Rattlesnake Ridge Trail. Fowler Trail goes straight ahead to reach a drift of wine-colored sandstone. It is hard not to be mesmerized by those climbing the sheer ramparts on the canyon's north side, but climbers on the south side face a unique challenge: The Bastille.

Continue to a set of interpretive signs featuring raptors, complete with sound and visual aids. A handy bench provides a good place to watch aerodynamic white-throated swifts dart through the air around the Bastille.

Farther along, an even steeper, higher rock tumble is topped by La Petite Bastille. A railroad cut allows passage through to the far side where wild hops grow. Gaze out to the eastern horizon before turning around to retrace your steps.

Enjoy the awesome rock formations of Eldorado Canyon State Park, best seen from the interesting and short Fowler Trail.

Doudy Draw

Trail Rating	easy
Trail Length	3.8-mile out-and-back
Elevation	5,900 to 6,100 to 5,850 feet
Amenities	Fenced-in parking
Highlights	a quiet draw, wildflowers
Location	Boulder Mountain Park
Directions	From central Boulder, take Broadway south (it becomes CO 93). Look for the Flatirons Vista Trailhead on the right, just south of CO 128.

Easy and scenic Doudy Draw Trail has a lot to offer hikers. Natural interests include ponderosa parkland, an array of mesa-top flora, a lush arroyo, and the Flatirons—great, red sandstone slabs of the Fountain Formation. Spring is a good time to visit, with wildflowers adding colorful notes. When cattle graze the tableland, flowers are sparse until you reach the gate at the draw's rim. From here, the descent offers plenty of wildflowers.

Parking for cars and horse trailers is usually adequate. Don't forget that thunderstorms often strike on summer afternoons.

After closing the gate at the trailhead, aim right along a gravel road as the trail sign indicates. Proceed around a curve, viewing pastureland until a west heading presents you with the jutting fins of the Flatirons in the distance. Composed of Ancestral Rockies deposition, and pigmented by iron-oxide, this 300-million-year-old formation was pushed into its present angle about 70 million years ago.

The track reaches a metal gate before rising on stony soil. Soon a glimpse of the Indian Peaks—quite photogenic when snow-creased in early spring—materializes through a canyon gap. Prior to passing through another gate, coast into a dip and continue traveling the flat, stony track. Here the road-way is accompanied by a giant power line that sometimes hums when the wind blows. Ponderosa pines dot the tableland and provide shelter for whisk-broom parsley and green gentian. When it reaches another gate, the trail narrows and the attendant power line veers off. Bluemist penstemon spreads in azure puddles under ponderosa pines.

A look down into Doudy Draw reveals a steep hillside and a pocket view of the snowfields on Indian Peaks. The track, hemmed by lush vegetation and peeled logs, drops into the draw, and the descent steepens over a rocky path where little pockets sport bright wildflowers. Early season hikers and equestrians may find a muddy track as they enter the draw itself. Opening like a stage curtain, the scenery in Doudy Draw makes proceeding worth a bit of mud. Listen for water sounds as you approach an entrenched creek trimmed with grassy banks. This is a great spot to pause for contemplation or a snack, and is the turnaround point for the description.

The trail does continue for another 1.5 miles or so until it arrives at the Doudy Draw Trailhead, just off Eldorado Springs Drive. You can leave a vehicle at each end of this trail, or trade car keys midway with another party for a through-hike. A paved path 0.4 mile from the Doudy Draw parking lot leads to wheelchair-accessible restrooms and picnic facilities.

Doudy Draw is a great spring wildflower walk, though its accessibility makes it nice in any season. Expansive scenery and a peek at Indian Peaks make this a winning close-in getaway.

Crescent Meadows

Trail Rating	moderate to strenuous (last few hundred yards)
Trail Length	5-mile out-and-back
Elevation	7,300 to 6,300 feet
Amenities	none
Highlights	South Boulder Creek finale
Location	Eldorado Canyon State Park
Directions	From the intersection of CO 128 and CO 93 south of Boulder, head south on CO 93 for 4.5 miles, then take CO 72 west for approximately 8 miles to Crescent Village. Turn right on Gross Dam Road and continue for 3 miles. Look for the trailhead and parking on the right, 0.2 mile after you cross the railroad tracks.

Crescent Meadows Trail proffers a modicum of solitude. Located in the far west sector of Eldorado Canyon State Park (disjunct from the main canyon headquarters), this trail provides a backcountry experience close to town. The hike descends 1,000 feet in 2.5 miles and extends from state park property into that of Boulder County's Walker Ranch Open Space. The hiker's reward, via a sharp, last-minute elevation drop, is a secluded spot on the banks of riverlike South Boulder Creek—a memorable finish for the trek.

Crescent Meadows Trail drifts down with the contours of the landscape's slopes and ridges. The trail reaches a set of steep well-crafted steps, and some of natural stone, which drop the hiker quickly to creek level.

Parking is usually adequate at the fenced area just 0.2 mile beyond the railroad tracks. It is common for thunderstorms to strike on summer afternoons, so be prepared.

Head east, accompanied by early wildflowers, a view of the distant Continental Divide, and the concrete face of Gross Dam. A trail kiosk points to Crescent Meadows Trail on the right (south).

Open slopes characterize the first portion of the hike, which drifts down through grasslands topped off by the tracks of Denver and Rio Grande Railroad. Ponderosa pines stud the hills, and flowers color their flanks. Decomposed granite forms a well-drained path that contours to the east among native shrubs.

Worn granite outcrops lead hikers toward a peek at the shark-tooth formations that define Eldorado Canyon. Beyond, Boulder Valley unfolds. A northern exposure nurtures Douglas firs before turning to drier habitat where the trail leads to a saddle crossing.

Wild roses and Canada violets bask in a shady ravine. Look for a state park sign warning mountain bikers of dangerous conditions ahead. Follow the lay of the land as the trail reaches another small saddle. A burned area beyond reminds us to be mindful of the danger of forest fires.

Pass a sandstone wall and enjoy another view of the sharp formations that compose Eldorado Canyon. Soon the song of flowing water reaches the hiker. For a brief stint, granitic outcrops make the route rocky and challenging.

Cruise along this backcountry sector until the crux of the hike arrives with a warning sign: no horses; bikers dismount. The next segment heads down—really seriously down. The trail builders accomplished an engineering feat, allowing the hiker to descend a steep, rather precipitous, section of trail by way of a series of shaded log steps and rock. Nearly spiraling in an effort to reach the water in as quick a manner as is safe, these steps—some knee-high—are to be treated with respect.

Carving a tight gorge out of stubborn granite, Boulder Creek, almost a river by Colorado foothills standards, sings a green siren song inviting you to enjoy its work of ages. Wildflowers and flowering shrubs, such as spring-blooming boulder raspberry, adorn the crevices in the rock.

Dip your feet into the meltwaters of the high country for a wildly cooling sensation—an icy reward after 2.5 miles of hiking in this bit of secret backcountry.

South Boulder Creek (South)

This hike accesses South Boulder Creek Trail from the south—a less-traveled route. The trail leads down to the rushing beauty of South Boulder Creek and drops 700 vertical feet in just 0.75 mile. The return qualifies as a fairly challenging uphill—perhaps more so for ascending mountain bikers than for those afoot.

Eldorado Canyon State Park contains two very diverse sections, the famous rock-climber's mecca on the east side and the lesser-known hiker's and biker's paradise on the western edge. In addition to a section of South Boulder Creek Trail administered by the state park system, visitors travel through property known as Walker Ranch, administered by Boulder County Open Space.

Decomposed granite and bedrock line most of the steep sections of the 1-mile trail as it descends into the canyon of South Boulder Creek. Follow the bold drop to river level where the trail turns east on an old railroad bed for 0.25 mile. A pair of riverside picnic tables mark the end of this hike.

Parking at the fenced trailhead, shared by Eldorado Canyon State Park's Crescent Meadows Trail, is adequate. Keep alert for gathering thunderstorms on summer afternoons.

As you head east from the parking area through a wildflower-strewn flat, a sign appears with an area map to orient you as to the trail configuration. South Boulder Creek Trail aims straight ahead on an east heading.

Corkscrewing down around shaded S-curves, the trail leads to a sign that indicates South Boulder Creek is 0.75 mile farther. Golden granite eroding into gravel requires hikers to watch where they place their feet. A brief

Trail Rating	moderate
Trail Length	2-mile out-and-back
Elevation	7,300 to 6, 600 feet
Amenities	none
Highlights	riverlike South Boulder Creek
Location	Walker Ranch, Boulder County Open Space
Directions	From the intersection of CO 128 and CO 93 south of Boulder, head south on CO 93 for 4.5 miles, then take CO 72 west for approximately 8 miles to Crescent Village. Turn right on Gross Dam Road and continue for 3 miles. Look for the trailhead and parking on the right, 0.2 mile after you cross the railroad tracks.

respite from downhill travel comes with a rustling aspen copse and a widening route.

Yet another sign tells of the change from Eldorado Canyon State Park land to Walker Ranch Open Space property and outlines the regulations. Then it's down again, reaching into the drainage where you will soon hear rushing creek sounds.

In a few tricky places, granite outcrops bulge underfoot. Across the canyon, black snags bear witness to the 1990 Olde Stage Fire—a contrast to the sylvan landscape traversed so far. The fire jumped the wide creek below and raged its way into the next section of trail. Wildflowers have begun the healing process by covering the affected slope with fresh foliage and, more importantly, soil-binding roots.

Broad turns take hikers to the banks of riverlike South Boulder Creek, where firs and spruces tower over the clear, rushing waterway. A turn upstream finds a path that parallels the creek. A short way up, you might find a small sweet bench that provides a shaded spot to rest and refresh. Perhaps you will see a water ouzel fly by or land on a river rock to glean an underwater meal.

After crossing a sturdy footbridge in the scenic canyon, the route follows an old railroad bed, providing a welcome flat surface as the river flows lustily below. The landscape along the roadbed is spattered with wildflowers. The north-facing riverbank is draped with a beautifully composed hanging garden featuring emerald mounds of alumroot. Downstream, water sluices through a rock-bound gap.

A pair of waterside picnic tables sit on the right, perfect for a shady snack break. Just down the trail, a tiny tributary flows from the northwest. The trail leaves the river here, making this a good turnaround point.

Convenient but far-away feeling, the deep reaches of beautiful South Boulder Creek are yours on this short hike with an aerobic return.

Golden Area

Golden, just west of Denver on US 6, is home to the Colorado Mountain Club and the American Mountaineering Center. It's no surprise that great hiking awaits nearby. In fact, the Golden area is a mecca for day-hikers, particularly those who enjoy exploring the foothills and montane life zones.

This region includes Golden Gate Canyon State Park, with its 14,000 acres of forest and parkland coursed by trails—some for hikers only. Every fall, the park's aspen population puts on a colorful show that metro-area residents need travel only a short distance to witness.

A handful of Jefferson County Open Space Parks lie in this region as well, such as White Ranch, Mount Galbraith, and Apex, featuring everything from steep rocky climbs to saunters through cottonwood copses. And the little stretch of green in the community of Wheat Ridge is a perfect spot for a quick escape. You'll find foothills hiking at its best, as well as some fun forays in the low(er)lands, along this easily accessed stretch of the Front Range.

Wildflowers splash color on this boulder-strewn slope at White Ranch.

Contents

Golden Area

Hikes 29 – 40

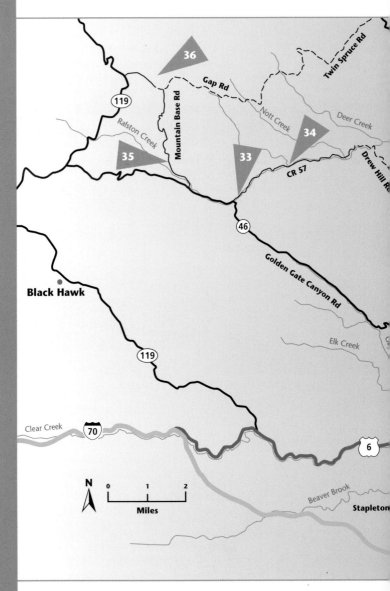

Twin Spruce Rd

Gap Rd

119

Mountain Base Rd

Ralston Creek

Nott Creek

Deer Creek

36

34

35

33

CR 57

Drew Hill Rd

46

Black Hawk

Golden Gate Canyon Rd

Elk Creek

119

Clear Creek

70

6

Beaver Brook

Stapleton

N

0   1   2

Miles

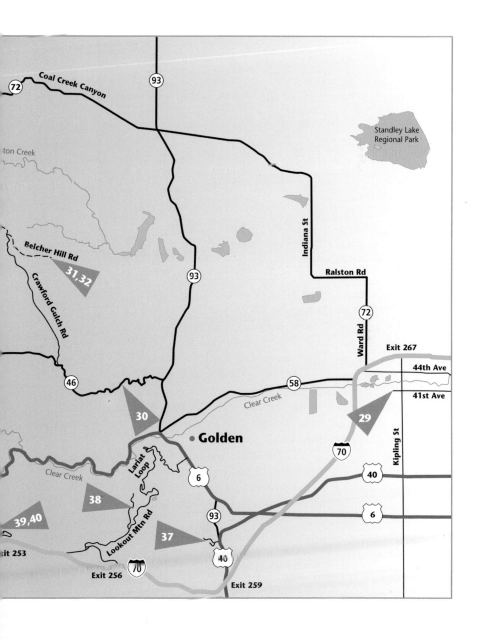

Hike 29

Clear Creek

This hike in Wheat Ridge Greenbelt West invites you to delve into a bit of suburban "wilderness," where birdsongs and creek-sounds replace the roar of traffic. Several small lakes soothe the senses and supply lucky anglers with largemouth and smallmouth bass. Bird-watchers might want to bring binoculars to view winged residents and visitors. Covered picnic tables are placed here and there along the way—perfect for dining alfresco.

The level trail winds through shady groves along Clear Creek, coming to Bass and West Lakes before arriving at busy Youngfield Street. The route backtracks to a bridge, then loops north of the creek and returns, via another bridge, to the segment upon which you began.

Parking in the dirt area of the Miller Trailhead is adequate. You can park at the large paved Youngfield Plaza if you choose to reverse the hike. Summer thunderstorms may pay an afternoon visit.

The Miller Trailhead, in the west section of the Wheat Ridge Greenbelt, serves both the crusher-fines hiking trail and the concrete bike path. Begin on the wide natural-surface trail, flanked by milkweed during the summer. Milkweed is the primary food source for monarch butterfly larvae, and a few of the orange and black adults may be flitting in the vicinity.

Traveling under mature trees such as cottonwoods, willows, and box elders, the companionable path passes inviting benches. Foxes frequent this wild-in-the city place. Be aware that occasional patches of poison ivy might appear along the way.

Trail Rating	easy
Trail Length	3-mile out-and-back with center loop
Elevation	5,300 feet
Amenities	restrooms at west end (Youngfield Street)
Highlights	a bit of "wild in the city," fishing ponds
Location	Wheat Ridge Greenbelt
Directions	From central Denver, head west on I-70. Exit south on Kipling Street, continue to 41st Avenue (a sign says dead end), and make a right. Proceed 0.3 mile to the Miller Trailhead and parking area.

A bridge spanning Clear Creek accesses Prospect Park; this is the same bridge you'll cross on the loop's return. For now, continue straight ahead and remain on the south side of the stream. Abundant prickly seed clusters of wild licorice claim the floodplain, as does a small cattail marsh.

An extensive cattail zone surrounds pretty Bass Lake. A tall patch of feather reed grass hides a park bench with a great view. Watch fish jump and waterfowl fly from this charming vantage point. Beyond the shimmering surface, North Table Mountain's bluff-like profile foregrounds the foothills of the Front Range.

Continue west along the north shore of Bass Lake, then along West Lake's shore. A "yield" sign beside another bridge forewarns walkers of the merging bike path.

This multi-use path is paved and cruises west to reach the trailhead and parking area at Youngfield Street. Restrooms and a water fountain are available here. Note that the fountain is a freeze-proof design, and it is necessary to press the button for a while before the water rises to the spout.

After checking the map sign, retrace your steps eastward along West Lake, watching for big blue herons, cormorants, and other water birds. When you arrive at the first bridge over Clear Creek, cross the span to access Tabor Lake. You'll be on the bike path now; turn right along this lake's open south shore.

Shaded once again, the path reaches the west side of Prospect Park. A trail to the left leads through an arbor entryway to a small habitat garden. Return on a path bisecting the park and head east toward Prospect Lake. A fishing float offers a nice view of the water. In front of the picnic pavilion, another arc-shaped bridge leads back across the creek, and a turn to the left retraces your incoming route back to the Miller Trailhead.

This western portion of Wheat Ridge Greenbelt is a great place to go "wild" in the city.

Cedar Gulch/Mount Galbraith Loop

One of the newer additions to Jeffco's ambitious and valued Open Space program, Mount Galbraith was the first park to be designated "hiker-only." Cedar Gulch Trail and the Mount Galbraith Loop make for an ideal outdoor workout. Add scenic value, and you have a perfect combination of natural beauty and aerobic exercise. Spring and early summer also bring on a good selection of foothills wildflowers.

The Cedar Gulch Trail angles up steadily toward the Mount Galbraith Loop, which wraps around to a crest. The descent on the north side includes a steep set of rock stairs. Sturdy footwear is recommended. Mount Galbraith is exposed for a goodly portion of its 4.2-mile balloon loop, requiring hikers to watch for building thunderstorms on summer afternoons. Parking on fine weather weekends fills quickly. Trail brochures are available at the kiosk.

The route begins by crossing Tucker Gulch on the Cedar Gulch Trail, then eases up along the south bank's open bench with views of narrowleaf and plains cottonwood trees. Switchbacks and stone steps weave through Douglas firs and turn the trail from a west heading to an easterly direction.

You'll follow the contour of an open slope of scrub and xeric plants such as prickly pear cactus, creeping mahonia, and yucca. The narrow angled track brings Table Mountain into view and rises past Rocky Mountain maple, waxflower, and ninebark shrubs.

The trail curves to the north, enabling the hiker to enjoy a respite under Douglas firs before reaching an exposed outcrop, crested on rock steps, where north Golden comes into view. Native bunchgrasses keep the steep slopes from eroding as the track approaches an outcrop wall. Here, the trail leads over a shelf transporting the hiker in the direction of a ravine. Mountain mahogany bushes and ponderosa pines open to expose a saddle below to the left, revealing the Coors facility. Sometimes the odor of fermenting beer wafts up here.

The Mount Galbraith Loop goes left or clockwise at the "T" intersection, and bypasses a neighborhood connector trail that spurs off of the loop. Soon, evergreens offer a pool of shade, followed by a view of North and South Table Mountain with Coors steaming in the middle.

The 180-degree view from the ridgeline runs from Boulder, to the north, around to the red roofs of Colorado School of Mines and its giant white "M" on Lookout Mountain. As the trail heads west, the Continental Divide comes into view. Below, a Clear Creek tunnel draws attention before the trail pitches up to a pink granite outcrop. This is a great place to pause before S-curving ruggedly back down again.

Evergreens shade the trail as it descends on decomposed granite. The steepest pitch sends hikers down a serious series of rock steps. The trail reaches a saddle before meeting up with the start of the loop again. From here, retrace your steps back to the parking area.

Close to civilization, but above and beyond it, this loop on Mount Galbraith is a winning getaway.

Trail Rating	moderate
Trail Length	4.2-mile balloon loop
Elevation	6,000 to 7,150 feet
Amenities	restroom
Highlights	hikers only, views
Location	Mount Galbraith, Jefferson County Open Space
Directions	From CO 93 in Golden, head west on Golden Gate Canyon Road (CO 46/CR 70) for 1.3 miles. The trailhead and parking are on the left.

Rawhide/Wrangler's Run Loop

Once the hunting grounds of Arapaho and Ute Indians, White Ranch Open Space proffers diverse habitats from ponderosa parklands to riparian areas and meadowed slopes. Near the trail's onset, there is a display of antique farm implements, perhaps used by the ranching White family. Ranches like this one kept the land from being developed, so today we can enjoy 4,200 contiguous acres in this Jefferson County Open Space Park. This route on Rawhide Trail and Wrangler's Run connects 2.4 of the nearly 20 miles of trail available.

Parking is in a large area shared by mountain bikers and picnickers. Summer afternoons are the time to watch out for building thunderstorms.

From the northeast corner of the main parking area, head left on Rawhide Trail. You'll pass a flat area of wildflowers and grasses as well as antique farm tools including a hay rake and a manure spreader. Continue to a pair of facing benches. Soon after, Rawhide Trail heads left in the general direction of a craggy rock formation—the Ralston Buttes.

Trail Rating	moderate
Trail Length	2.4-mile loop
Elevation	7,450 to 7,120 feet down
Amenities	restrooms, picnic tables
Highlights	foothills ranchland, wildflowers, old farm equipment
Location	White Ranch, Jefferson County Open Space
Directions	From CO 93 in Golden, head west on Golden Gate Canyon Road (CO 46/CR 70) for just over 4 miles to Crawford Gulch Road (CR 57). Turn right, continue for approximately 5 miles, and make another right onto Belcher Hill Road. Proceed 1.8 miles to the east parking lot.

Before Rawhide Trail enters ponderosa pines, xeric wildflower species decorate an area of arid rocky soil. A sign announcing a geologic point of interest marks a short trail leading to an unusual outcrop, intriguingly crosshatched with fossil-like inclusions.

Just beyond the entrance to the spur, the main trail puts you at a junction with Longhorn Trail across the way. Turn left to continue on Rawhide Trail. As the trail curves down through spaced pines, bright blooms catch the eye, including purple swatches of summer-blooming monarda or beebalm.

The trail now pitches down quite steeply through long-needled ponderosas. Most steep trails, including this segment of Rawhide, use a series of water bars for erosion control. These bars also help slow the gravity-propelled momentum of hikers heading downhill. Watch the footing as the trail launches into its 300-foot descent. When the dry pine habitat turns lush with willows and grasses, you know you are nearly down.

The loop turns left on Wrangler's Run at the junction, and as the track narrows it parallels a small watercourse. Wildflowers dot the riparian zone, and, in autumn, colors glow with the changing leaves of dark-barked river birch, willows, and an occasional quaking aspen.

When it meets the Rawhide Trail again, Wrangler's Run is flanked by jointed horsetails, more correctly called smooth scouring rush. The loop turns left onto an old ranch road and gently regains the 300 feet it lost. Wildflowers await nectar-seeking bees and butterflies as the road wends its way up past pines and rocky outcrops to the hike's end.

While multi-use White Ranch has almost 20 miles of trails, Rawhide/Wrangler's Run Loop makes a fine introduction to the park and features a number of habitats in just 2.4 miles. Views of Denver and the Plains can be enjoyed from pine-shaded tables—a perfect spot for a picnic.

Longhorn/Maverick/Sawmill/ Mustang/Belcher Hill Loop

Tucked into rolling ponderosa parkland in the foothills west of Golden, White Ranch is one of many gems in Jefferson County Open Space. Once a cattle ranch operated by the White family, this 4,000-plus-acre park provides nearly 20 miles of scenic trails. Trail names included in this 3.8-mile loop reflect the area's history.

Though the elevation gain appears to be just a few hundred feet, a number of gains and losses put this loop into the moderate category. In other words, exercise is a major component of the hike. Ample parking is available. Be alert for fat-tire aficionados and gathering thunderstorms.

A trail kiosk kicks off the initial Rawhide Trail portion of the loop. Antique ranch equipment that might have served the White family rests in flower-spattered grassland as the trail proceeds toward convenient restrooms. Continue east alongside picnic tables to a sign pointing out Longhorn Trail. Curve around to another sign where Longhorn heads right for a gentle descent across a sloping meadow. Table Mountain's long escarpment appears to the east.

Narrowing for a rough little switchback, the trail allows for distant views of Denver's metro area and the vast plains beyond. Continuing down the slope through pines, pass an outcropping before a sharp right turn takes the loop from Longhorn Trail onto Maverick Trail.

Maverick Trail curves into one of Mother Nature's rock gardens—bright with primary hues. Dip into a ravine before rising on log water bars to travel the north bank of a seasonal micro-creek. A shady ascent brings the hiker into

Trail Rating	moderate
Trail Length	3.9-mile loop
Elevation	7,500 to 7,800 feet
Amenities	restrooms, picnic tables
Highlights	antique farm equipment, views
Location	White Ranch, Jefferson County Open Space
Directions	From CO 93 in Golden, head west on Golden Gate Canyon Road (CO 46/CR 70) for just over 4 miles to Crawford Gulch Road (CR 57). Turn right, continue for approximately 5 miles, and make another right onto Belcher Hill Road. Proceed 1.8 miles to the east parking lot.

open terrain for a gentle segment of trail. Erosion diversions across the track lead to lichen-covered rocks before an S-curve further elevates the route under stately ponderosa pines.

A view of Ralston Buttes, to the north, is the reward for the next incline. Maverick Trail reaches a junction where the loop briefly turns uphill to the right, following Belcher Hill Trail. Soon a three-way intersection appears, and the route turns left on Sawmill Trail. (A sign indicates that there's a camping area in 0.6 mile.)

Wander along the old ranch road among soughing pines, and be on the lookout for grouse. With its discreet coloration and noisy flight, the plump, duck-sized grouse might startle you. But it is the red, yellow, and black plumage of the western tanager that will really astound you. Scan the trees for these brightly colored birds.

Curve up into the open backcountry camping area. To the east, downtown Denver anchors the edge of the Great Plains while to the south, the view stretches clear to Pikes Peak.

Open-skied shrubland begins where Sawmill Trail narrows and ragged granite breaks the skyline. One-third mile past the campground, the loop takes a right on Mustang Trail and is lifted by log water bars. Switchbacks border rugged outcrops where the track ascends more steeply, and the route returns to the ponderosa belt and on up to a blessedly flat section.

A bench precedes a fork where the route turns onto the Belcher Hill Trail and heads downhill. After dropping some 300 feet, the wide entrance road is reached. Cross it and access a pleasant part of the loop that takes off downhill about two-thirds of the way into the parking area. This connector trail swings around, traveling 0.7 mile back to the start of the route. Curve down through aspens to find open skies nurturing a wildflower rock garden. The trail heads right when it reaches an old ranch road, and travels through a wide skied meadow to the parking and picnic area.

This loop within White Ranch Open Space features views, soughing pines, and wildflowers, and provides a chance for some good exercise.

Horseshoe Trail to Frazer Meadow

Golden Gate Canyon State Park has some elbow room with 14,000-plus acres and 35 miles of trail to explore. The 1.8-mile hike to Frazer Meadow features a ramshackle log building. Traveling by a creek lined with blooming things, pretty Horseshoe Trail gradually takes hikers up to a wide meadow in the shadow of Mount Tremont. Freshness comes in the form of montane scenery, seasonal abundance of wildflowers, and the very air itself. The handsome visitor center provides information on this trail and others in the park, and features a beautiful deck that overlooks a pond.

The trail steadily ascends, then hits a brief rough pitch before easing along to enter level Frazer Meadow. The addition of Rim Meadow Loop extends the hike through more wildflower-carpeted scenery. Refer to a park map or ask at the visitor center for more information. Parking at the trailhead is somewhat limited. Secure a spot by arriving early, and you might also avoid summer afternoon thunderstorms.

Trail Rating	easy to moderate
Trail Length	3.6-mile out-and-back
Elevation	8,160 to 9,080 feet
Amenities	restrooms
Highlights	stream, wildflowers, historic building
Location	Golden Gate Canyon State Park
Directions	From CO 93 in Golden, head west on Golden Gate Canyon Road (CO 46/CR 70) for approximately 14 miles to the visitor center. Turn right onto CR 57 and continue to the Frazer Meadow Trailhead on the left. There is a fee to enter the park.

Posted with a route map, the sign for Horseshoe Trail to Frazer Meadow aims hikers across a little creek flowing in the dappled shade of quaking aspens. Riparian vegetation thrives along the waterway, as do butterflies nectaring on a wide variety of wildflowers.

The trail continues to ascend, passing lichen-speckled outcrops and holding to the narrow drainage as it heads up to a small footbridge. A stiff, rocky, switch-backed pitch follows, but fortunately it is fairly brief and mostly shaded.

Returning to its gradual nature, Horseshoe Trail forks left at a junction. Hikers will find this trail's celebrity in a colorful selection of wildflowers. The dancing shade of aspen leads to the deeper shade of spruce, nurturing white monkshood. Blue columbine, designated as Colorado's state flower in 1899, adds graceful beauty to the ongoing flower-scape.

A plank bridge crossing leads to a rough trail segment before leveling through a vale of rainbow petals. This visually inspiring scene invites you to relax. Find a boulder to sit on and admire Mother Nature's unparalleled gardening talent.

It isn't long before Horseshoe Trail bisects the deep grasses of Frazer Meadow. The expanse is anchored by an old log building—its broken-down wooden bones a testament to this meadow's historic past. Mount Tremont's 10,200-foot peak rises above wildflower-spattered grasses and shrubby cinquefoil bushes. Legions of evergreens march up the mountain's sloping shoulders. Once you've taken in the beauty here in Frazer Meadow, retrace your steps back through nature's colorful bounty.

Hiking Horseshoe Trail to Frazer Meadow is tantamount to waltzing with wildflowers as they dance along the creek, bow in deep conifer shade, and sweep the aspen glens with their colorful attire. Find satisfaction along this stretch of trail that lifts body and spirit in Golden Gate Canyon State Park.

Forgotten Valley

Surrounded by 14,000 acres of diverse habitat, fishing ponds, picnic areas, and campsites, Golden Gate Canyon State Park's impressive trail system has something for everyone. The trail to Forgotten Valley not only gleams with wildflowers, but, upon reaching an 1870s homestead overlooking a pond, provides a thoughtful glimpse into the park's past. The route also leads hikers through diverse ecosystems.

Before tackling Forgotten Valley Trail, make a stop in the attractive visitor center to peruse the bookstore and excellent displays. Pamphlets highlighting the park's history, mammals, birds, and wildflowers are also available. The outside deck features a trout-pond exhibit.

Parking, shared by picnickers, is spread out among several paved areas near the trailhead. Arrive early for a spot and to avoid thunderstorms that might brew up on summer afternoons.

The Burro Trail, marked with the animal's hoof print, leads hikers under ponderosa pines to a map signboard, then over a bridge spanning Ralston Creek. The trail swings left along the stream where a sign indicates the way to Forgotten Valley. On the north side of the creek, an open hillside features a colorful array of wildflowers.

Follow the post with burro tracks up the south-facing slope, and then continue along a dry drainage of mixed conifer and quaking aspen. Rocky footing ensues as the trail lifts hikers, passing a dip. A forested mountain view appears to the south as the flat and sandy track enters ponderosa parkland.

A junction sends the route left along Mountain Lion Trail. A lodgepole pine stand is fringed by intensely blue mountain penstemon. Back under ponderosas, frequent posts keep you on the right "track"—follow the lion's paw print. The wide gentle trail eases down by aspens accompanied by the pleasant sound of birdsong and running water.

After crossing a chatty little creek, the track soon rises. Forgotten Valley unfolds, revealing a serene pond with an old homesteader's cabin on the far shore. You will return to this scenic spot after completing the short keyhole segment of the hike.

Head north on the continuation of Mountain Lion Trail. An evergreen groundcover, kinnikinnick thrives along the bank of the road. On the left, dappled in aspen shade, a brook girded by willows nourishes a meadow of riparian wildflower species.

A left turn onto the Buffalo Trail is identified by a bison's hoof print. Cross a tiny waterway where you might find hot pink shooting stars. Moving on, the two-track trail's gravelly soil leads you around to complete the keyhole. Within sight of the weathered homestead, the level trail crunches along on golden decomposed granite. Buffalo Trail angles sharply left as it wraps around back to the pond, passing a wild rose garden.

The narrow track saunters along a sloping flowery meadow toward the cabin. The building once belonged to Anders Tallman, who immigrated from Sweden in 1869. A farmer and rancher, Tallman converted it from a schoolhouse to his family home, which it remained until the 1950s. Tallman Ranch is now listed on the Colorado State Register of Historic Places. Please respect the warning signs at the historic structure.

Close-in, yet far away in feel, flowery Golden Gate Canyon State Park is a treasure. Put yourself in a place of serene scenes and great color, and try the satisfying and varied trek to Forgotten Valley.

Trail Rating	easy to moderate
Trail Length	3-mile out-and-back (with keyhole)
Elevation	7,800 to 8,200 feet
Amenities	restrooms, picnic area
Highlights	1870s homestead, pond, wildflowers
Location	Golden Gate Canyon State Park
Directions	From CO 93 in Golden, head west on Golden Gate Canyon Road (CO 46/CR 70) for approximately 14 miles to the visitor center. Turn right onto CR 57 and continue for 2.5 miles to the Bridge Creek Trailhead on the left. Parking is adjacent to the road. There is a fee to enter the park.

Elk/Coyote

A premier place for abundant wildflowers and grand scenery, Golden Gate Canyon State Park is a great destination surprisingly close to the Denver metro area. The park's montane-life-zone habitats support an impressive array of recreational opportunities for outdoor enthusiasts, including some three dozen miles of trail. One of the easier and shorter routes on this trail network is the hike on Elk and Coyote Trails from Ole' Barn Knoll to Bootleg Bottom. Summer blooming wildflowers color the landscape on this gentle hike. Be sure to stop and peruse the interpretive displays at the attractive visitor center, pick up a park map, and pay the park entry fee before heading up Mountain Base Road.

Elk Trail gradually ascends through meadowland, damp areas, and glades to top out at a junction where it meets Coyote Trail. It then drops and crosses a riparian area before ascending to Bootleg Bottom on Mountain Base Road.

Parking is usually available until the weekend lunch bunch arrives to claim the slots near picnic sites. An early start may help you to avoid those wild and crazy summer afternoon thunderstorms that can arrive with little notice.

Wildflowers, such as warm-hued wallflower, speckle the south-facing grassy slope that leads Elk Trail down from the picnic area at Ole' Barn Knoll. Passing the remains of old log buildings, the track turns north along a riparian zone. Here the moister left side of the trail supports species such as tall Jacob's ladder, while the drier right is favored by penstemons and paintbrush.

Trail Rating	easy
Trail Length	2.2-mile out-and-back
Elevation	8,160 to 8,800 feet
Amenities	restrooms, picnic sites
Highlights	meadow walk through wildflowers
Location	Golden Gate Canyon State Park
Directions	From CO 93 in Golden, head west on Golden Gate Canyon Road (CO 46/CR 70) for approximately 14 miles to the Visitor Center. Continue for just over 1 mile to Mountain Base Road and turn right. Park at Ole' Barn Knoll on the left. There is a fee to enter the park.

A natural rock garden in the filtered shade of a quaking aspen copse sets hikers off toward a small footbridge. The path leads from open grassy spaces into a boggy zone filled with willows and moisture-loving plants such as snowy meadow anemone. Farther up the trail, wild iris colonize in the shade of aspens. These smooth, white-barked trees also nurture purple monkshood.

Climbing a bit more brings you into a mass of bright wildflowers resembling a shattered rainbow come to rest. At peak bloom, around the 4th of July, look for more than two dozen different flower species here. The route turns right onto Coyote Trail at the junction in the midst of this colorful display. Hikers wade through lush grasses under stately aspens to cross a tiny stream. Moisture-lovers, such as big-leaved cow parsnip, flourish in the filtered shade and damp soil here.

The vegetation quickly changes from lush leafy things to ponderosa pines as the trail rises onto a long dry traverse. Mountain Base Road leads to Bootleg Bottom Picnic Area. From here, return to the trail's start by retracing your steps.

Golden Gate Canyon State Park is an outdoor enthusiasts' mecca, loaded with grand scenery, great hikes, and numerous wildflowers. An easygoing jaunt on Elk and Coyote Trails promises a wonderland of wildflowers that can be enjoyed both out and back again.

Raccoon Loop

Trail Rating	easy to moderate
Trail Length	2.5-mile loop
Elevation	8,800 to 9,250 feet
Amenities	visitor center, restrooms
Highlights	100-mile view of the Continental Divide, wildflowers
Location	Golden Gate Canyon State Park
Directions	From CO 93 in Golden, head west on Golden Gate Canyon Road (CO 46/CR 70) for approximately 14 miles to the Visitor Center. Continue for just over 1 mile to Mountain Base Road, turn right, and proceed 3 miles to the information office and trailhead at Reverend's Ridge Campground. There is a fee to enter the park.

Golden Gate Canyon State Park, about 15 miles northwest of Golden, boasts over 14,000 acres threaded by 35 miles of hiking trails. This special park, just a stone's throw from Denver's metro area, offers varied terrain and activities including fishing ponds, scenic picnic areas, and campgrounds. It also boasts wondrous wildflowers.

The limited parking lot at Reverend's Ridge is shared by camper facilities. Alternately, you can park at Panorama Point and hike the loop from here. An early start makes parking easier and optimizes chances of beating summer afternoon thunderstorms, which can brew up quickly. Park brochures are available at the handsome visitor center.

Lodgepole pines flank the trail as it heads out from the northeast side of the campground and amphitheater. Curving down through mixed woods, Raccoon Loop follows posts imprinted with its namesake's paw print. The trail bottoms out in a small drainage, then ascends steadily, switchbacking through sparsely vegetated forest, to reach a fabulous view.

From Panorama Point overlook deck, visitors' eyes sweep 100 miles of Continental Divide. This vista, centered by the Indian Peaks, including 13,397-foot South Arapaho, 13,502-foot North Arapaho, and 13,409-foot Navajo, is memorable. To the north, 14,259-foot Longs Peak graces the landscape.

Raccoon Trail resumes to the right of the restroom on the east side of the parking area, and travels through evergreens via an entrenched section. It closely encounters a road before heading left, and continues down to meet overhanging willows. A big blue spruce shelters a rich wildflower garden. The path weaves through aspens and thick meadow grasses before arriving at a small footbridge.

As the trail curves west, lush riparian habitat gives way to a drier landscape. Look ahead for a glimpse of the distant Continental Divide. The cruising path narrows, leading to a hairpin curve where footing is less stable. Continue down to where aspens gain in girth, showcasing large-flowered clumps of elegant blue columbine.

An S-curve bends the narrowing trail down through smaller aspen. A flowery slope graces the view before the Indian Peaks portion of the Continental Divide again steals attention. The loose and stony track drops through mixed forest, leveling in an aspen glade where water sounds please the ear. Again, descent calls for careful footing. Conifers give way to robust aspens and a wealth of columbine. The path bridges the elfin creek again.

The trail passes through a small willowed meadow, home to a private cabin, and into mixed forest. Head around to the right and follow an old road designated with a white arrow. Arrive at a sign with a raccoon's paw print, sending the route left and uphill. Easygoing now, the trail leads through aspen to a four-way junction. Head right to complete Raccoon Loop. After an uphill trudge, find yourself back at Reverend's Ridge Campground.

Early summer is the time to catch the wildflower show along Raccoon Trail. This hike rates high, with a wide-angled, snow-peaked vista, a sweet creek, and lots of columbine.

Apex/Pick 'n Sledge/ Sluicebox Loop

Apex Open Space is a lovely surprise. With a humble beginning adjacent to Heritage Square Amusement Park/Shopping Center, Apex Trail quickly leads to a ravine threaded by a small creek. An ancient Indian village was once located here; much later the same spot became the head of a toll road to Gregory Diggings, now known as Central City.

The 4.5-mile loop pushes into a ravine before a right turn sends it climbing, later to level out a thousand vertical feet above the trailhead. It then drops over switchbacks to complete the balloon portion, before rejoining the string back to the parking area. Parking is generous, but an early arrival will help hikers beat thunderstorms on summer afternoons.

On the northwest edge of the lower parking lot, pick up a guide to Apex Park at the metal box, then head west under orphan elms. Turn right onto a rusted bridge, then take the first dirt path on the left bearing a sign for Apex Trail.

As the trail heads up Apex Gulch, wildflowers color the short grassland. Following the sound of running water, the track ascends past polished leaves of poison ivy—leaves of three, leave them be. On the right in front of an interesting rock outcrop, a big wooden sign is emblazoned with a trail map of Apex Park. Take a moment to note the Apex/ Pick 'n Sledge/Sluicebox Loop featured in this description.

After a brief meeting with the creek, Apex Trail rises over rocky ground until it comes to a junction where the loop angles up to the right, onto Pick 'n Sledge Trail. The track climbs quickly across a dry south-facing slope. At last, the trail levels a bit, reaching a panoramic view of the

Trail Rating	moderate
Trail Length	4.5-mile balloon loop
Elevation	6,150 to 7,150 feet
Amenities	restrooms
Highlights	diversity of terrain and ecosystems, wide-ranging views, wildflowers
Location	Apex Park, Jefferson County Open Space
Directions	From Denver, take I-70 West to Exit 259, and get on US 40 heading east. Bear another left onto on Heritage Road (CR 93) and make another left into the trailhead and parking area, about 150 feet before the fire station. Park by northeast corner of paved area.

Denver-metro area. The distant cityscape is flanked by Green Mountain on the right and Table Mountain on the left. Great patches of knee-high little bluestem bunchgrass anchor the stony soil. The trail switchbacks toward the west again and big bluestem grass—often waist-high—converges in colonies.

Following a switchback, the trail continues its ascent, becoming rockier. This sun-struck trail segment reveals glimpses of the city and the Great Plains beyond. Take another moment to gaze northeasterly to the horizon, where a long white shape sits like a solitary range of permanently snow-capped peaks—Denver International Airport.

The track eases a bit, and sounds of civilization disappear as the route continues past a few lonely ponderosa pines, and turns up a switchback onto a southwest-facing slope. Where Grubstake Trail junction arrives, continue this loop on Pick 'n Sledge Trail. Rocky and rising, the track heads up to the next switchback, after which the footpath levels. Douglas firs, which prefer north-facing slopes, greet the hiker with welcome shade before the trail crosses an open slope.

The track broadens as it starts its shady way down to another junction, where the loop angles left onto Sluicebox Trail. A number of switchbacks take the track through boulder raspberry shrubs and pines. Sluicebox Trail drops quickly below the ponderosa pine belt to rejoin Apex Trail, where the loop heads downstream. Legions of butterflies enjoy the creek, including little blue melissas "puddling" at every damp spot to quench their thirst for moisture and minerals.

Under narrowleaf cottonwoods, Apex Trail touches the creek, passing a large rock outcrop on the left. Travel through extensive thickets of wild plum, hawthorn, and chokecherry, following Apex back to the parking area.

Close-in Apex Park's varied plant communities and wide vistas await your discovery.

Forest and Meadow Loops

Perched on top of the mountain of its namesake, west of Golden, Lookout Mountain Nature Center and Preserve is a great venue for families and nature lovers. The first-rate nature center is an extraordinarily beautiful example of building with recycled materials, including train boxcars, soda bottles, and auto windshields. Jefferson County Open Space Parks has done itself proud here, with a site-perfect building aptly described by a volunteer as the "Elegance of nature recycled." Helpful staff and volunteers offer information on naturalist-led activities at Lookout Mountain Nature Center and Preserve, as well as at other Jeffco parks. In addition, several short trails lead under ponderosa pines and open skies. In spring, wildflowers entertain.

Parking becomes more competitive on weekends as well as when the Boettcher Mansion is hosting an event. Keep in mind that summer afternoons may host thunderstorms.

Head south from the nature center on a nice shaded path toward the Boettcher Mansion. Bear left of some picnic tables to find a map kiosk featuring the Forest and Meadow Loops. These two loops together form a figure eight of sorts.

Beginning on Forest Loop, dominated by ponderosa pines, the trail curves south of the mansion, until the route turns left at a junction. As you wander along the pine-flanked path, you might spot the elusive Abert squirrel. This dark, often black, tuft-eared squirrel is most likely seen under or in the long-needled ponderosa, which serves as both his room and board.

The smooth path now comes to a footbridge where a sign says Meadow Loop. Take a moment to enjoy a pine-shaded bench at the beginning of the loop, or choose the seat in a copse of young quaking aspens farther along. It is interesting to note that aspens have pretty much the same life span as humans do—rather fleeting for a tree.

The open meadow features grasses mixed with seasonal wildflowers. Views of the Denver cityscape and the endless plains beyond juxtapose man and nature. As the trail rounds the sunny meadow and heads back, the vanilla-scented bark of bigger ponderosas welcomes you to the second part of Forest Loop. Wend gently uphill to another wooden footbridge.

The loop leads back to the Nature Center where a notebook of wild-flower photographs is available to peruse. Hikers will be able to identify some of the flowers encountered on the Forest and Meadow Loops. Several activity rooms in the nature center invite exploration, and the unique lifelike displays ask for close inspection.

Lookout Mountain's Forest and Meadow Loops make for an ideal hike close to the Denver-metro area. Don't miss the splendid visitor center, and, if plans can be made ahead of time, take part in a naturalist-led activity.

Trail Rating	easy
Trail Length	1.4-mile double loop
Elevation	7,540 to 7,430 feet
Amenities	visitor center, naturalist-led activities
Highlights	handsome "recycled" visitor center and exhibits, city view, 1917 Boettcher Mansion
Location	Lookout Mountain Nature Center and Preserve, Jefferson County Open Space
Directions	Take I-70 West from Denver to Exit 256, and turn right. You'll see a sign (brown and white) for Lookout Mountain Nature Center. Follow a series of such signs to the gated entrance.

Braille Nature Trail

Brief, informative, and unique Braille Nature Trail is administered by Denver Parks and Recreation's Mountain Parks system. The specially designed hike loops a small spring-fed creek and features a plastic-covered guidance cable. Thirty-one interpretive signs in both print and Braille make it an unusual and valuable trail. For the sight-impaired, a careful descent is advised, and a clockwise hike might be considered as the west side of the loop is smoother.

Just west of the Bison Herd enclosure, a gravel access road leads to the trailhead. The counterclockwise description here descends 190 vertical feet on the southwest-facing slope and returns on the cooler north-facing bank.

Parking is competitive on summer weekends. An early start ensures space and might also help you avoid thunderstorms on summer afternoons.

Begin the loop on the right at a sign explaining the formation of the Rocky Mountains. Wildflowers color the way. Indian-named kinnikinnick, a creeping subshrub related to manzanita, likes the dry shade of ponderosa pines and the lithic soil underneath them. Look for this evergreen ground-cover as you approach a broad bench on the right, from which you can glimpse the Continental Divide. A sign explains the significance of the dividing of the waters—west to the Pacific Ocean and east to the Gulf of Mexico.

The narrowing path continues down over uneven footing. A smooth black cable leads the way to an interpretive sign about ponderosa pine. Turning to the tree, take a deep whiff of the crevices in the reddish-orange bark. Is it vanilla you smell? While the aroma is pleasant to humans, it reportedly deters insects.

Trail Rating	easy
Trail Length	1-mile loop
Elevation	7,400 to 7,200 feet
Amenities	outhouse, picnic sites at bottom of trail
Highlights	forested trail with interpretive signs in Braille
Location	Genesee Park, Denver Mountain Parks
Directions	From Denver, take I-70 West to Exit 253 (Chief Hosa). Turn right and then right again onto Stapleton Drive. Continue 1.1 miles, bearing left at the fork, to the trailhead at a closed gate on the right.

As the track continues downward, it's bisected by an old logging road that interrupts the guidance cable for a few feet. Soon an intimate open meadow, dotted with small quaking aspens, offers a west-facing bench upon which to relax. Thanks to a variety of wildflowers, the colorful meadow is a favorite place of bees, butterflies, and hummingbirds.

The last interpretive sign on this side of the loop helps visitors to recognize the difference between the needles of a spruce and those of a fir. Fir needles are flat and friendly while those of spruce are spiky and stiff.

At the bottom of the trail is a level area with a couple of picnic tables. Uneven stepping-stones challenge the hiker as the trail approaches a footbridge where the loop turns left. The cable resumes before the uphill return, passing clumps of dark-barked river birch. The loop advances in the shade of tall evergreens. Wildflowers, appreciative of moist growing conditions, thrive on the northern exposure.

Take time to read the signs about weather influences while you stroll through the shade. As someone sagely noted: Climate is what we expect, weather is what we get.

The path arrives at a wooden bench cantilevered out over the minuscule spring-fed creek. This is a nice spot to sit and contemplate nature. Shade graces the rest of the loop as you head up toward the parking area.

Take time to enjoy an interpretive hiking experience in Denver's backyard. This intimate walk in the woods is just a few minutes from the freeway, yet feels a world away.

Beaver Brook West

With quick access from Denver's metro area via Interstate 70, Beaver Brook West is a convenient place to hike. The west trailhead, under the auspices of Denver Mountain Parks, takes hikers down along a shady 1.5-mile route to reach babbling Beaver Brook. For those looking for a longer hike, this trail continues for a total of about 7 miles. Hikers on Beaver Brook Trail trace a route that was once used by Indians. Delightful wildflowers paint the way.

Parking on summer weekends gets creative in the two small carparks adjacent to the signed trailhead. Thunderstorms are likely on summer afternoons, so be prepared.

The first 0.3 mile of this hike travels along Braille Nature Trail. Coated with tough black plastic, a sturdy cable installed for non-sighted explorers leads off on the right. This segment, attended by a series of interpretive signs that include an explanation in the raised dots of Braille, leads to the Beaver Brook Trail. Travel on lithic soil to arrive at a bench on the right, where a distant view of the Continental Divide is nearly obscured by conifers. Edge down along the cable to a sign discussing the uses of juniper's soft, blue berries (actually, cones). Another sign highlights the familiar and delicious vanilla scent of summer-warm ponderosa pine bark.

Trail Rating	moderate
Trail Length	3-mile out-and-back
Elevation	7,400 to 6,600 feet
Amenities	outhouse, picnic sites at bottom of Braille Trail
Highlights	trail ends at cool clear Beaver Brook, wildflowers
Location	Genesee Park, Denver Mountain Parks
Directions	From Denver, take I-70 West to Exit 253 (Chief Hosa), turn right, and then right again onto Stapleton Drive. Continue 1.1 miles, bearing left at the fork, to the trailhead at a closed gate on the right. Take the right-hand trail.

The cable is interrupted by an old stage road, but resumes a couple of strides later. The trail drifts into a soothing pocket of aspen where a bench sits near a seasonal waterway. Next up, a sign defines nearby conifers: Fir needles are friendly and flat, while those of spruce are spiky and square.

A couple of picnic tables come into view as the route turns left to Beaver Brook Trail. Pick your way down very uneven rock steps and cross a footbridge. A turn to the right after the bridge sends hikers down Beaver Brook Trail. Watch for occasional tree-mounted squares lettered BB to keep you on course. Evergreen shade creates a pleasant feel as the route is escorted by lush vegetation.

More shade comes along as the track gently declines into a nursery of Douglas firs before the contour of the landscape brings the trail onto a rugged canyon hillside. The gradient drops on uneven stone steps to the small creek draining Bear Gulch. A spruce with a BB sign on it invites you to pause by the clear brook.

Decomposed granite paves the path as it leads to a mossy area and descends on stone stairs before undulating into an area of charcoal gray rock. Turning west, you begin a steeper descent into Beaver Brook's rugged canyon. Rocks and roots underfoot call for caution.

Gold and silvery-gray lichen encrust a sheer outcrop where the route— note the BB sign—takes a firm right and drops fast on stone steps. The track evens and the ear picks up more vigorous water sounds.

Moss-hung rock leads to a couple of switchbacks on the way to a formidable cliff face. Here, a shelf of rock becomes the trail bed for a brief stint. Another BB sign aims you down to cool your feet in clear Beaver Brook.

Be sure you've brought plenty of water for the uphill return trip. At the footbridge turnoff, continue straight ahead on the west side of the creek, where you'll find the guiding cable and interpretive Braille signs again.

A fine close-in hike convenient to I-70, Beaver Brook Trail leads hikers on an informative adventure to lively Beaver Brook.

I-70 West

Beguiling peaks and posies lure hikers on the Herman Gulch Trail.

The I-70 corridor winds through the Front Range of the Rockies west of Denver, accessing a treasure trove of trails along the way. These high-country hikes boast the wondrous scenery and diversity that make them appealing to Colorado residents and visitors alike.

This collection of routes features everything from walks among the remnants of Colorado's colorful mining days to strenuous climbs through alpine tundra up to boulder-strewn summits. The Continental Divide borders this region, and from its eastern flanks hikers can experience staggering views of sky-piercing peaks, icy mountain lakes, and brilliant wildflower displays. The southernmost glacier in the United States, St. Mary's, lies in this region, as does the highest paved road in North America, which leads through the Mount Evans Wilderness to the top of its namesake fourteener. This wilderness, designated in 1980 under the Colorado Wilderness Act, offers numerous trails through its 74,401 acres that are only open to foot traffic.

Contents

I-70 West
Hikes 41 – 57

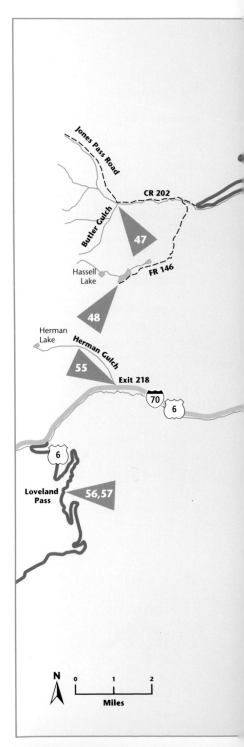

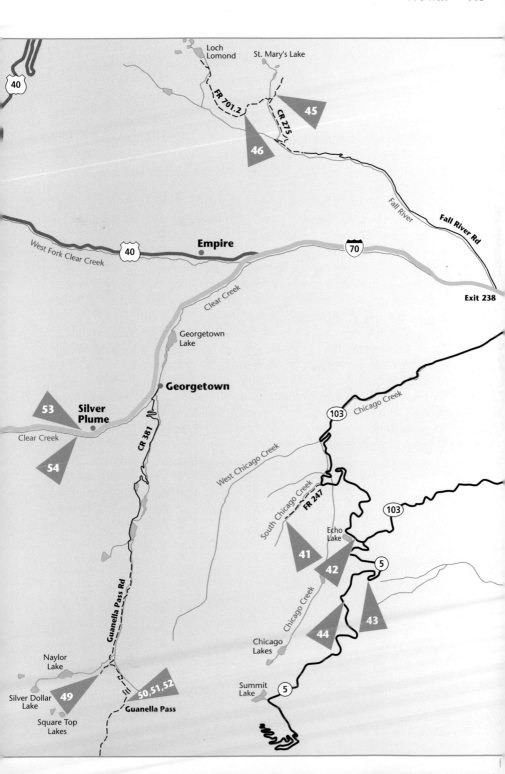

Loch Lomond

St. Mary's Lake

40

FR 701.2

CR 275

45

46

Fall River

Fall River Rd

West Fork Clear Creek

40 **Empire**

70

Exit 238

Clear Creek

Georgetown Lake

Georgetown

Chicago Creek

103

53 **Silver Plume**

Clear Creek

CR 381

West Chicago Creek

South Chicago Creek

FR 247

103

54

Echo Lake

5

41

42

43

Chicago Creek

44

Guanella Pass Rd

Naylor Lake

Chicago Lakes

49

Silver Dollar Lake

50,51,52

Summit Lake

5

Guanella Pass

Square Top Lakes

South Chicago Creek

South Chicago Creek Trail, in Mount Evans Wilderness Area, feels like a trek to the back-of-beyond—a steady climb into remoteness. If solitude is valuable to you, this trail may be one to try. It is also an access for climbing Gray Wolf Mountain. The gradient of South Chicago Creek Trail knows only one word: up. With a 1,300-foot elevation gain, be prepared to go aerobic all the way.

Parking at road's end, where the South Chicago Creek Trail begins, is casual but usually adequate. With high peaks to the west, be prepared for summer afternoon thunderstorms.

A decent road leads you past a number of summer cabins to its end at a sign for Mount Evans Wilderness. Take a moment to check out the quote from the Wilderness Act of 1964: "Where the earth and its community of life are untrammeled by man, and man himself is a visitor who does not remain."

Just north of the parking area, evergreens and willows shelter South Chicago Creek. For the first part of the trek, as you start your climb toward the west, creek-sounds may be discerned through the forest.

The north-facing drainage slope upon which the trail travels begins with a damp area where pink elephant heads find shelter under willows. Decomposed granite underlies the next segment, leading to a small wilderness sign. After a deteriorating section of corduroy-like road, where logs laid side by side once conveyed wagons over boggy areas, the track rises, becoming rougher. It is a wonder wagons ever made it up this rocky and ruggedly pitched roadway.

Trail Rating	moderate to strenuous
Trail Length	5-mile out-and-back
Elevation	9,960 to 11,300 feet
Amenities	none
Highlights	a trek in solitude
Location	Mount Evans Wilderness, Arapaho National Forest
Directions	Take I-70 West from Denver to Exit 240 in Idaho Springs. Head south on the Mount Evans Highway (CO 103) for 6.7 miles to FR 247. Turn right and proceed 0.8 mile, take the right fork, and continue 0.6 mile (crossing a small creek) to the signed trailhead.

From the left, a clear rivulet waters wildflowers, offering a bright spot in the midst of dense forest. Spruce is joined by lodgepole pine, and the sparse understory consists mostly of dwarf broom huckleberry. In wet years, mushrooms of many species pop up near the trail.

Another section of decaying corduroy road appears—a harbinger of more rocks and steep grades ahead. At last the gradient eases long enough for hikers to take a look at the myriad mosses and lichens populating this north-facing exposure.

Solitude is the reward for a rough, rugged, and rising trail, as the slash of sky overhead is defined by a conifer corridor. An area of downed timber obliterates the old wagon road, and a detour easing left circumvents the downfall. Patches of grass accommodate a level breather before another corduroy road segment leads toward more open forest. A huge slash-pile marks the site of an old sawmill along with a pair of wood-fueled ranges that once heated workers' meals. Curving around the far side of the woodpile, the fading roadway wends up to glimpse thick willow carr through the trees on the right.

The trail winds up on singletrack now, giving the hiker wider glimpses of the meadow to the north. Only cairns and bits of trail lead you toward the partly open skies and the thickly vegetated meadow. Here and there, flows of angled rocks cross the waning path. Perseverance is what this hike is about. At tree line, 13,602-foot Gray Wolf Mountain finally comes into full view, having been as secretive as the animal for which it is named.

For a remote-feeling wilderness experience, give this less-frequented trek a try. South Chicago Creek Trail satisfies explorers' expectations.

Hike 42

Lower Chicago Lake

Discovering Lower Chicago Lake is like finding a sparkling ten-acre emerald. Set within a circlet of pewter peaks, this enchanting alpine lake is your reward, for the trek to Lower Chicago Lake can be a taxing one. Hikers descend over 400 feet before beginning the main ascent, having to regain that elevation at hike's end. However, it is not as arduous as it sounds—the switchbacks are gradual and shaded. Boots are highly recommended; hiking poles are handy too.

Early arrival is advised, not only to secure a parking place at Echo Lake spur road's end, but also to avoid the wild thunderstorms that can arrive with lightning speed on summer afternoons.

From the east side of the cul-de-sac parking area at the end of Echo Lake's entrance road, a cabled gate sports a sign for this Denver Mountain Park. Head up to the picnic area and find Echo Lake before you. Turn right to locate a small sign pointing the way to Chicago Lakes Trail. Follow the

lakeshore briefly before a sign on the right shows the way to Chicago Lakes.

Rise shortly, then drift down to rise again over a rocky path. Snatch glimpses of the distant mountains between the conifers. Granite ledges on the steep, west-facing exposure support bristlecone pines, mats of moss saxifrage, and clumps of alumroot. The colorful maw of 14,265-foot Mount Evans' massive face opens to the south.

Jumbled rock accompanies you as the trail takes on a backcountry feel.

Trail Rating	moderate to strenuous
Trail Length	10-mile out-and-back
Elevation	10,600 to 10,800 to 10,360 to 11,420 feet
Amenities	restrooms, picnic sites
Highlights	very scenic, lovely alpine lake, wildflowers
Location	Mount Evans Wilderness, Arapaho National Forest
Directions	Take I-70 West from Denver to Exit 240 in Idaho Springs. Head south on the Mount Evans Highway (CO 103) for 14 miles to the Echo Lake entry road on the right. The trailhead and parking area are at the end of this road.

Undulating under rugged outcrops, the track reaches a small national forest boundary sign. Make your rocky way down to a series of long switchbacks that carry you to Chicago Creek. (You have descended some 400 vertical feet lower than the ridge you ascended earlier.) Along the amber-bedded stream, summer brings water-loving wildflowers, such as tall chiming bells, into bloom. Sturdy half-logs facilitate the creek crossing.

The trail leads to a road. Turn left, follow it 1 mile up to the Idaho Springs Reservoir, and continue along the west side of this impounded lake. At the far end, Chicago Lakes Trail returns to singletrack with a sign announcing Mount Evans Wilderness.

The trail climbs into a burned area that extends most of the way to Lower Chicago Lake. Aspens, as well as abundant forbs, have set the healing process into motion among myriad standing snags. The path alternates between stretches of climbing and level track, burned and unburned land. Chicago Creek's water-talk babbles from beneath a shade of dense willow carrs, and great cliffs of sheer granite, topped with treeless tundra, rise into the sky. The track takes on rocks, and sometimes roots, as it gains elevation.

A cruising section of trail, through standing and downed snags softened by wildflowers and healthy grasses, is a pleasant change. So is the waterway crossed on convenient stones.

The way eases through a forested section before entering an open area surrounded by towering mountains. Despite the great heights, the scene is intimate. Behold Lower Chicago Lake shimmering in its verdant bowl under the rugged brows of lofty summits. When you're ready, head back the way you came.

The varied 5-mile trek to Lower Chicago Lake is spectacular, but the lake itself is the hike's true jewel.

Mount Goliath Lower Interpretive Loop

Trail Rating	easy, but at high elevation
Trail Length	0.25-mile loop
Elevation	11,540 feet with slight elevation gain
Amenities	information center, restrooms
Highlights	sweeping views, alpine wildflowers
Location	Mount Goliath Natural Area, Mount Evans Wilderness, Arapaho National Forest
Directions	Take I-70 West from Denver to Exit 240 in Idaho Springs. Head south on the Mount Evans Highway (CO 103) for 14 miles to Echo Lake and turn right onto CO 5. Continue for 2.9 miles to the Lower Loop Trail on the left. (The Upper Alpine Loop is 1.9 miles farther up on the left.) There is a fee to drive on the CO 5 portion of Mount Evans Highway.

Mount Goliath (also known as Goliath Peak), on which this trail is located, is a sub-peak of the Mount Evans massif. Walk the Lower Interpretive Loop at 11,540 feet, then drive up some 600 vertical feet to the Upper Alpine Loop at 12,152 feet, described in the hike following. For those so inclined, the Upper and Lower Loops are joined by a rugged connector trail, making a steep but beautiful mile-long hike. Both loops offer a wealth of easily accessed alpine wildflowers. In addition to natural terrain, the Lower Loop contains what is reportedly the world's highest man-made rock garden. And the views are marvelous.

Parking in the Lower Loop's lot is generous. Plan to arrive early to absorb the extensive mountain vistas and avoid wild summer afternoon thunderstorms. Winds are possible at any time, so dress for changeable weather.

From the parking area, head right on crusher fines to begin the Lower Loop. Aim for a crystalline freshet on the left that flows between angular granite boulders harboring many alpine plant species. Alpine-rock-garden enthusiasts envisioned this scenic spot as a convenient place to study tundra plants, and the carefully sculpted granitic garden is one of a kind. Wander around this unique rock garden, then return to the main path.

Curve around to Mother Nature's untamed idea of a granite garden, and examine tundra gems such as sweet-smelling alpine rock jasmine. Coming up on a tiny rivulet, bend down to sniff fragrant, rosy-purple charming wallflower. Look nearby for more, which can be cinnamon- or buff-colored. The pattern of daring wildflowers planted by Mum Nature juxtaposes the human-hand planted side of the trail, though natives thrive in both places.

Continue west, pausing at an interpretive sign that discusses the 1,500-year-old bristlecone pines before you. Short stiff needles flecked with white resin and nascent cones as purple as plums are diagnostic characteristics. Twisted and ribboned with age by a harsh environment, the venerable bristle-cone pines are something to think about—certainly a lesson in tenacity. What was man up to when these patriarch pines were seedlings?

A fork in the trail sends the described loop left; the right fork climbs a rugged route a mile or so to top out where the upper loop begins. The left fork drifts through ancient pines and Engelmann spruce to return to the open. Legions of forested slopes foreground a serigraphy-like vista clear to the Great Plains, concluding the Lower Loop.

Mount Goliath's easily accessed Lower Interpretive Loop provides a gentle opportunity to acquaint yourself with alpine wildflowers and see amazing bristlecone pines. The views from the Mount Goliath Natural Area, which is accessed by the highest paved road in America, are simply stunning.

Mount Goliath
Upper Alpine Loop

The Upper Alpine Loop on 12,214-foot Mount Goliath offers easily accessed tundra wildflowers. Explore a natural rock garden full of alpine gems set in splendidly rugged terrain. The trail, which shares part of its path with the M. Walter Pesman Trail, is short and not too difficult, but hiking boots are a good idea. It's hard to keep your eyes on the ground when the vistas are simply stupendous.

The Upper Loop is only 0.5 mile around, but the elevation and rough nature of the trail qualifies it as moderate in difficulty. At 12,000 feet there is approximately 35 percent less oxygen than at sea level.

Parking for the Upper Loop is limited. Plan to arrive early to secure a spot and to avoid wild summer afternoon thunderstorms. High winds are possible at any time, so dress for capricious weather. Note that for every 1,000 feet of elevation gain, temperatures drop 3 to 5 degrees. If it is 70 degrees in Denver, it may be only 40, possibly windy, degrees at the Upper Alpine Loop Trailhead.

Trail Rating	moderate
Trail Length	0.5-mile loop
Elevation	12,152 to 12,200 feet
Amenities	none
Highlights	sweeping views, tundra wildflowers
Location	Mount Goliath Natural Area, Mount Evans Wilderness, Arapaho National Forest
Directions	Take I-70 West from Denver to Exit 240 in Idaho Springs. Head south on the Mount Evans Highway (CO 103) for 14 miles to Echo Lake and turn right onto CO 5. Continue for 4.8 miles to Upper Loop Trail on the left. There is a fee to drive on the CO 5 portion of Mount Evans Highway.

Head to the north end of the pull-through parking area to access the trail. Start to the left at the interpretive sign explaining the M. Walter Pesman Trail, and set off on the loop clockwise.

Mother Nature has perfected rock gardening in this alpine life zone. Buns, mats, and cushions of vegetation cling to the gravely soil, offering their gemlike blossoms in the latter part of June and into early July. Wildflowers here have a 6–8-week summer window in which to complete the cycle of emerging, budding, blooming, betting on fertilization, and seed-setting and dispersal.

As it rises through craggy granite outcrops, the trail weaves a rocky course among alpine floral jewels. On the way to a curve, a grand sweep of the Continental Divide is exposed. Snow-furrowed peaks mark the western horizon. To the southwest, and in closer proximity, the Mount Evans massif and its jagged Sawtooth arête command the skyline.

Rise over natural rock and coil up through a tight passage between a pair of rough, gray granite boulders. Head for a saddle where lichen-encrusted outcrops lead the way from a west aspect to an eastern exposure. After a hairpin curve, the narrow pathway levels. Beyond a slope of bleached, gnarled bristlecone pine snags and their dark-needled living brethren, a panorama stretches as far as the eye can see. Ease along a lithic path in the company of flowers and tufted-grass. Your vehicle is just around the corner.

Convenient to pavement and not too taxing despite the lofty elevation, the Upper Alpine Loop of the M. Walter Pesman Trail is an extraordinary experience. Not to be missed at prime bloom-time, this charming hike highlights the wonders of high-altitude wildflower adaptation, with magnificent vistas to boot.

St. Mary's Glacier and Lake

Trail Rating	moderate to strenuous, but brief
Trail Length	2-mile out-and-back
Elevation	10,400 to 10,800 feet
Amenities	none
Highlights	scenic alpine lake, "glacier" remnant
Location	Arapaho National Forest
Directions	From Denver, take I-70 West to Exit 238. Go north on Fall River Road to the St. Mary's Glacier sign, and park in the pullout on the left, just beyond the trail. The trailhead is on your right as you walk back down the hill, and marked by a tall sign: "Glacier Hike."

You will feel as if you have discovered a secret alpine treasure—well-earned due to the short but rugged hike that puts lovely St. Mary's Lake at your feet. Just west of Idaho Springs, and roughly 24 miles from Denver, Fall River Road lifts you into the high country world. With a towering, wildflower-splashed cliff sheltering the persisting glacier, and granite boulders interspersed with ancient bristlecone pines in the foreground, St. Mary's Lake is picture perfect.

The 400-foot elevation gain is accomplished in only 0.75 mile along a trail that is rocky and serious about ascent. Of course, the fact that the hike begins at some 10,400 feet also means you're in for some aerobic exercise.

Parking on summer weekends gets creative, though weekdays should be fine. Pay particular attention to the parking signs here. Attention should also be paid to another summer phenomenon: afternoon thunderstorms that can build with amazing rapidity. Climbing to the upper portion of St. Mary's Glacier leaves you totally exposed to the elements, requiring extra care.

From the parking pullout, walk back down the road several hundred feet to a fenced derelict building where a rugged roadway takes off uphill to the right. A tall sign indicates this is the route of the "Glacier Hike." Although the way is steep and rough, legions of hikers have made a fairly decent path that avoids much of the jumble of rock.

The trail gives hikers the chance to glance at the mountainside's lingering snowfields before arriving at a junction. Stay left on the rugged uphill fork. Evergreens populate the sides of the trail, leaving the cobbled roadbed open to the skies. A second junction sends the trail left again, and a rocky knob appears.

Lodgepole pines, along with spruce, bristlecone pines, and a few aspens, flank the route as it approaches a weatherworn gray stump on the right. Turn right as the hike heads east. A short level stretch of trail weaves through a boulder field that looks as though gnomes swept the flat earth before carefully dropping granite chunks on it.

At last, ascend through more granite boulders and gnarled bristlecone pines and prepare yourself for lovely St. Mary's Lake. Cradled by flower-strewn cliffs, worn granite outcrops, and that stubborn accumulation of ancient snow misdeemed a glacier, the gemlike lake is a justly earned reward. Birdsong might soar through the air, perhaps in the wake of a mountain bluebird—azure as a clear Colorado sky.

Crossing the outlet's arced bridge takes you above the lake to climb on the east flank of the glacier. The melting snout of the diminishing snowfield nurtures a variety of subalpine wildflowers. While admiring their colors and forms, consider the shrinking snow. Will it someday be gone?

You'll feel a sense of achievement, not to mention a lift of spirit, as the beauty of St. Mary's Glacier and Lake surrounds you.

Loch Lomond

Loch Lomond sounds romantic—a bonny lake with a Scot's name. Chaperoned by 13,250-foot Mount Bancroft, and James Peak at 13,294 feet, the lake sits just east of the Continental Divide. Weekends see increased traffic as four-wheelers jolt up the access road. For hikers, the trek is sometimes rocky, mostly uneven, and serves up a tricky creek crossing along the 2 miles to the lake. Sturdy hiking boots are helpful.

Taking care to respect private property, park on the west side of Alice Road just before it intersects with Upper Forest Road. An early start might help you finish the hike before summer afternoon thunderstorms build to a light-and-sound show best viewed from your vehicle.

Ascending through lodgepole pine forest, the trail sets off west on Forest Road 701.2. Becoming stony underfoot, the track leads through limber pine and bristlecone pine. To tell the trees apart, examine the cones. Limber's are elongated, and their rounded scale-ends are smooth. One touch of a bristlecone gives away its prickly nature, and resin-flecked needle bundles are also telling characteristics.

Increased gradient rewards you with a skyline view far to the southeast, punctuated by fourteener Mount Evans. Old mining sites add to the scene. The route levels but becomes rockier as it passes a tailing pile where saucy chipmunks and larger golden mantle ground squirrels frolic. Spruce and fir soon supplant lodgepole pines.

Trail Rating	moderate
Trail Length	5-mile out-and-back
Elevation	10,360 to 11,200 feet
Amenities	none
Highlights	majestic mountains, lake
Location	Arapaho National Forest
Directions	From Denver, take I-70 West to Exit 238. Go north on Fall River Road for 8.4 miles. Turn left on CR 275 and set your odometer at 0. Continue heading straight at mile 0.15, straight at mile 0.55, bear left at mile 0.7, and right at mile 1.05 to reach access road FR 701.2. Park on the side of the road, respecting private property.

Stunted aspens and flagged spruce surround a sign indicating FR 701.2. Wildflowers accent the vistas as you continue up where jumbled granite finds a tumbling fork of Fall River. Quartz intrusions swirl and ribbon the granitic rocks, and Mount Eva and Parry Peak, both over 13,000 feet, come into view.

Paralleling the bright-water creek, the road comes upon cobbles underfoot, requiring careful boot placement. A broad ford makes crossing a bit of a challenge, but it can be done on boulders just downstream. After crossing, keep right on the main track.

Up a bit, among conical spruces, the way levels and passes primitive campsites. On the left, a hide-and-seek stream waters a verdant meadow. Curve up to the west to reach a color-splashed hillside and cross the creek, which, this time, passes under the road, not over it. The winding roadway climbs past boulder-studded meadows and the tumbling creek. Stunted and contorted by prevailing winds, the spruce have shrunk into green walls of krummholz. Ascend to a barren expanse, looking more like a parking lot than a road. Rugged pewter rockscape and ragged peaks form Loch Lomond's granite basin.

The jeep road ends at the west side of the lake, but a footpath continues through willow and spruce. The flowers keep coming as the trail, hemmed by vegetation, grows muddy underfoot. Hikers must execute fancy footwork when crossing seeps and rocky rills. But the best is yet to come on this colorful adventure.

Stay to the outside through grayed conifer trunks as you follow a section of poorly defined trail. An open overlook allows hikers to take in the view. Glistening water cascades into the lake from the towering wall on the far side.

The stimulating 2.5-mile trek to Loch Lomond offers exercise and fresh, if thinner, air. Grand peak views, water music, and beautiful wildflowers contribute to a sense of peace and accomplishment.

Butler Gulch

A prime hike, Butler Gulch Trail is not only floriferous, but scenic and full of adventure. This beautiful trek, located west of Berthoud Pass Road off Jones Pass Road, climbs to a wide-open bowl cradled by the Continental Divide. Altitude and elevation gain combine to give Butler Gulch its moderate to strenuous rating. With stream crossings, rugged tread, and steep pitches, boots are really de rigueur.

Parking is extremely limited, so arrive early. Additionally, the goal cirque is above tree line and exposed to wild thunderstorms on summer afternoons.

Walk around the big gate at Butler Gulch's start on an old roadway. Cross high above a rushing creek and enter a droopy-boughed forest. Along the eroded rising track, pocket openings offer glimpses into lush meadows. The rocky ascent continues to a stream, where crossing can be interesting.

On the far side of crystalline Butler Creek, the trail heads up and to the left. Wildflower species abound here, such as tall chiming bells and blue columbine.

A meadow-scape daubed with rosy paintbrush soothes as you prepare to tackle a stiff pitch. Cascading rivulets and seeps accompany the rising trail's switchbacks. One such switchback reveals colorful 12,947-foot Vasquez Peak to the north, framed by a gap in the coniferous forest.

Trail Rating	moderate to strenuous
Trail Length	5-mile out-and-back
Elevation	10,400 to 11,640 feet
Amenities	none
Highlights	great subalpine wildflowers, creeks, Continental Divide views
Location	Arapaho National Forest
Directions	From Denver, take I-70 West to US 40 and head north. Turn left on Henderson Mine Road (CR 202) and continue for 2.5 miles to Jones Pass Road. Turn right and proceed 0.5 mile to the trailhead and parking area on the left.

Next on the beauty agenda is a moss-garden vignette. Seemingly planned with meticulous sophistication by Mother Nature, trickling water wends between emerald cushions—a master gardener's velvet coup.

Pockets of flowers appear on either hand as you rise on a rocky tread. Perseverance brings you into the glorious open, where waves of brilliant flowers welcome you to a basin. The sweeping peaks of the Continental Divide, snow-creased and majestic, create the mountainscape for which high country Colorado is justly famed.

Wondrous meadows, teeming with vivid wildflowers, inspire hikers to continue the easing ascent. Soon, the roadway becomes less defined, and alpine species such as moss campion and alpine sandwort root their tight cushions and mats in the lichic soil. Twinkling petals of pink and white accent the middle of the old road.

Talus slopes on the left nurture clumps of enchanting blue columbine, Colorado's state flower since 1899. These raw rock slopes are home to a little animal with a penetrating voice, the pika. Perky and round-eared, this member of the ancient order of rabbits and hares is always busily gathering vegetation for curing in winter hay piles.

As you climb higher into the semi-cirque, you'll be reacquainted with tumbling Butler Gulch Creek as it bisects the basin. Further exploration reveals a surprise—old mining relics of an era when miners thought nothing of pursuing precious minerals at 12,000 feet.

Challenging Butler Gulch Trail offers inspiring sights and water sounds, as well as wonderful wildflower offerings. Give this 2.5-mile trek a try, especially during late July's floral extravaganza.

Hassell Lake

Trail Rating	moderate to strenuous, but short
Trail Length	2-mile out-and-back
Elevation	10,500 to 11,335 feet
Amenities	none
Highlights	small lake, Continental Divide views
Location	Arapaho National Forest
Directions	From Denver, take I-70 West to US 40 and head north through Empire. Turn left on Henderson Mine Road (CR 202) and left again onto Woods Creek Road (FR 146). Proceed 1.3 miles to the fork and bear left. Continue for 2.5 miles to the trailhead.

Sitting in a broad bowl of Continental Divide mountains, pretty Hassell Lake offers a short but hearty hike to a scenic subalpine lake. Willow-studded meadowlands surround the lake, and wildflowers of many species color the way. The first half of the trek, accomplished while you are fresh and eager, is the steepest; the second half seems like a breeze. You'll pass two impounded lakes on the drive to the trailhead, making natural Hassell Lake a special destination. Boots are recommended, both for rocky pitches and watery stretches.

Parking is shared by those going to Urad Lake, and can be crowded on summer weekends. An early arrival will increase your chance of finding a parking place and help in beating summer afternoon thunderstorms.

At the high west end of Urad Lake, look for a bermed old road and the start of the trail to Hassell Lake. A short rise gives way to a path through a stand of conifers and a planked footbridge over a muddy section.

The next segment, on a dry south slope under open skies, gives you a sparkling view of Urad Lake. Shortcuts, created by unenlightened hikers, have scarred the earth along here, leaving the steep slope open to erosion and unsightly grooves of raw soil.

Continue switchbacking as small aspens and stalwart bristlecone pines usher in a challenging section. Vegetation is doing a steady, albeit slow, job of knitting the eroded banks together with creeping kinnikinnick and mats of whiproot clover. Stunted trees cling to the precipitous incline over which you climb. At last, the trail reaches a stone-studded level area, and the most strenuous effort is thankfully behind you.

Cool evergreen shade and the sound of tumbling water soothes, while a cascade refreshes water-loving wildflowers. Relax, as does the route, along the clear stream where the trail is cushioned by forest duff.

The trail fades into the lush vegetation as it nears Hassell Lake's outlet. Look for little pink elephants (elephant head) trumpeting the site of a pair of logs spanning the creek. After crossing, turn to the left and follow a path to the lakeshore.

From here, keeping the lake on your right, head for an open area that simply sings about snacks and maybe a snooze. Sitting in the sun by dancing Hassell Lake is the perfect trail's end.

Those who wish to explore the far shore, or even encircle the lake, must bushwhack. Nimble feet will keep boots dry if you stick to the high-ground hummocks that dot the boggy places. Willows shelter myriad subalpine wildflowers, such as star gentian.

This more adventuresome route may reveal delightfully sculpted miniature landscapes at your feet, like the one with a twinkling foot-high waterfall. Nearby, the keen-eyed may discover recumbent pink bog laurel. When you reach the tall willows, make your way on the up-side to cross a hidden creek. The next few inlets are spanned more easily. Trammeled spaces among conifers eventually open, revealing a trail that leads back to the outlet creek.

Hassell Lake sparkles in its plush subalpine setting like a small gem cradled in emerald velvet. The surrounding Continental Divide peaks complete the treasured scene, which serves as a just reward for your strong uphill effort.

Silver Dollar Lake

Silver Dollar Lake Trail has it all—short length, beautiful surroundings, wild-flowers galore, and, of course, the alpine lake itself. In spring hikers may encounter lingering snowbanks, but summer promises a colorful display of subalpine and alpine flowers. Although a few level spots offer breathers, almost 700 vertical feet are gained on the 1.3-mile trail to Silver Dollar Lake.

The mile-long spur road to the trailhead is rough, but experienced drivers can usually make it (high clearance is helpful). There is plenty of parking in the lower lot, where the spur road takes off from Guanella Pass Road. However, leaving a vehicle here adds 2 additional miles to the hike. On week-ends, the upper parking area fills with early arrivals despite its rough entry. An early start is a good idea, enabling hikers to complete the hike before summer afternoon thunderstorms strike.

A Silver Dollar Trailhead sign marks the start of the route, which leads through willows into typical subalpine flora such as pink-headed daisies, subalpine larkspur, and several kinds of senecio. The pathway winds up and approaches a little creek cooled by the shade of big spruces. The incline increases on its way to a small drainage where brookcress and knock-your-socks-off-pink Parry primrose grab the attention of early season hikers.

The path, still shaded, rises to cross a tiny outlet flowing from an inti-mate pond encircled by several wildflower species. Along a mineral-soil path, continue to a sunlit opening in the forest. Evening out before curving up, the track passes meandering social trails. Keep to the left to remain on Silver Dollar Trail.

Trail Rating	moderate to strenuous (due to high elevation)
Trail Length	2.6-mile out-and-back
Elevation	11,200 to 11,950 feet
Amenities	none
Highlights	alpine lake, countless wildflowers
Location	Arapaho National Forest
Directions	Take I-70 West to the Georgetown Exit (228). Follow signs for Guanella Pass. From the outer periphery of Georgetown, proceed 8.5 miles to a spur road on the right, about 0.2 mile past Guanella Campground. Park here, or proceed 1 mile on rough road to the trailhead.

As the track climbs, trees grow shorter and switchbacks take the trail—rocks, roots, and all—up into the open, passing a rockscape where the grade eases. Down to the right, a gargantuan pile of stones provides ideal habitat for the busy little pika, a tailless, rabbit-related charmer with a piping voice that carries across the rocky terrain. Round a corner to meet oddly appealing frosty ball or Hooker thistle—a flower that appears soft, but is actually prickly from nodding head to pale green base.

The trail comes upon a rocky ravine that may harbor a stubborn snowbank. Above, a dozen kinds of little wildflowers, such as alplily, snowball saxifrage, and chiming bells, flourish in snow-free zones. The track narrows by a bank with a mossy seep and launches into a fairly level section. Tundra wildflowers, such as sweet-scented clovers, wait to be admired.

A dip may harbor a persistent snowbank and perhaps even snow buttercup. From the dip, the trail crawls up a raw rocky slide where a view of privately owned Naylor Lake spreads out far below. In this harsh habitat, cushions of bright pink moss campion, mats of white alpine sandwort, and succulent rosettes of bigroot spring beauty make way for clumps of blue columbine. Downslope to the right, color sings through rosy paintbrush, blue chiming bells, and daffodil senecio.

Vegetation closes in as the trail grows rocky, heading toward a bright meadow. Continuing on, an inspiring view widens to a sweeping panorama of the Continental Divide. The path is friendlier underfoot for a while before it resumes its rocky rising. The track levels amongst thick turf grasses and patches of knee-high spruce krummholz before ascent takes over once again, pushing you on to reach Silver Dollar Lake. One last rise and the lake, pressed against the shattered flank of 13,794-foot Square Top Mountain, comes into view.

The trail to Silver Dollar Lake is a must for viewing mid- to late-summer wildflowers in the high country, and is one of the finest flower hikes on the Front Range.

Square Top Lakes

On top of Guanella Pass, directly across from the trail to Mount Bierstadt, is the scenic trail to Square Top Lakes. Two attractive lakes, both above tree-line, are found up this moderate trail. Additionally, the hike revels in flowers and mountainscape majesty.

Square Top Lakes Trail (also called South Park Trail #600) shares parking with several other routes. An early start ensures convenient parking, and helps hikers avoid summer afternoon thunderstorms.

The trail begins levelly across tundra where alpine wildflowers bloom early in the season. The rutted route descends—it will soon go up again. Cross a rich boggy area and travel a willow-flanked track.

The path ascends gently along a warm south-facing slope that supports a wide selection of wildflowers. Continuing up the often double-tracked trail, hikers travel on remnants of an old road once used to stock the lakes with trout. Pass along a slope alive with red paintbrush before reaching a small pond on the right. This might be a place to pause and watch for the white-crowned sparrow. This brave bird, with a black-and-white-striped cap, lays its pale bluish-green eggs in the tundra's harsh environment.

Up here, a rocky area may be home to the pika, whose shrill voice is bigger than he is. Though he looks like a rather charming rodent, the pika is a member of the ancient order that includes rabbits and hares. He is frequently heard, though less often seen. Watch for his "hay" piles drying for winter storage.

As the track wanders up, you might see another feathered denizen that frequents the Guanella Pass area: the ptarmigan. In summer this grouse sports such thoroughly mottled plumage that it could be mistaken for a lichen-encrusted rock. In winter its feathers are pristine white.

Trail Rating	moderate
Trail Length	3-mile out-and-back to Lower Lake
Elevation	11,700 to 12,050 feet
Amenities	none
Highlights	mountain majesty, alpine lake, tundra flora
Location	Pike National Forest
Directions	From Denver, take I-70 West to Exit 228 at Georgetown and follow signs for Guanella Pass. The trailhead and parking area are on the east side of the pass.

A steep ravine, filled with sharp-edged boulders, is home to clumps of lovely blue columbine. This spurred native often takes on rain-washed colors in the alpine zone, as it does here.

The path briefly becomes a bit boggy, but soon returns to open rocky ground. Listen now for cascading water on the left where Lower Square Top Lake's outlet sounds off. The first lake is just up ahead.

Ascend the last pitch to Lower Square Top Lake at 12,050 feet. This willow-lined, low-lipped bowl seems to be hanging like a sky-reflecting mirror. In the background, tipped on edge, is 13,794-foot Square Top Mountain. Plenty of moisture-loving wildflower species grow among the dense grasses and short willows near the water, such as satiny, dusky-purple star gentian. Plump marmots romp in the rocks above the lake.

An afternoon thunderstorm may precipitate your return to the trail-head, but clear skies call for the additional 250-vertical-foot climb to Upper Square Top Lake. On the return trip, the grandeur of Mount Evans and its connecting "sawtooth" ridge to Mount Bierstadt command awe.

Square Top Lakes are a definite destination for high-country aficionados. This hike is one of Denver's closest accesses to tundra landscape, and offers spectacular scenery and floral splendor.

Geneva Knob

The hike to Geneva Knob, just inside the Mount Evans Wilderness boundary, begins on the Rosalie/Geneva Mountain Trail. One of the easiest high-alpine hikes along the Front Range, the 2 miles to the rock pile dubbed Geneva Knob offers magnificent scenery. The trailhead, just off the southeast side of Guanella Pass Road, is easily accessed. The trail's moderate rating is not due to difficulty, but to high elevation, which significantly decreases available oxygen. You'll have approximately 35 percent less oxygen here, at roughly 12,000 feet, than you enjoy at sea level.

This route follows the Rosalie Trail for the first mile, then it diverges along an old wagon road to a saddle where the trail fades. Aim southwest toward 11,941-foot Geneva Knob and circle it counterclockwise.

Parking at the pass is generous but can be crowded on good weather weekends as hikers head out to bag Mount Bierstadt. This is thunderstorm country, so begin hiking early to avoid getting caught out on the treeless tundra.

The trailhead sign stands at the south end of the upper parking area. Execute a full turn to take in 13,602-foot Gray Wolf Mountain to the northeast; the imposing Sawtooth arête between 14,065-foot Mount Bierstadt and 14,265-foot Mount Evans to the east; Geneva Mountain to the south at 12,335 feet; and Square Top Mountain to the west, at 13,794 feet. Rocky Mountain majesty is yours.

With the grand bulk of Mount Bierstadt on your left, Rosalie Trail to Mount Geneva travels south through tundra, rising evenly as it passes myriad blooming gems. The growing season is extremely brief at this elevation. Alpine flora miraculously performs emergence, flowering, fertilizing, and seeding in what may be a 6- to 8-week summer window.

Trail Rating	easy to moderate (due to elevation)
Trail Length	4-mile out-and-back
Elevation	11,669 to 11,941 feet
Amenities	none
Highlights	Mount Evans Wilderness, Pike National Forest
Location	sweeping views, tundra wildflowers
Directions	From Denver, take I-70 West to Exit 228 at Georgetown and follow signs for Guanella Pass. The trailhead and parking area are at the pass.

A sign directs hikers onto trail #603 toward wind-battered Engelmann spruce that form a krummholz (German for crooked wood) island. The cluster's windward side, nipped in the bud, gives it a "flagged" appearance. Keeping a low profile in order to conserve energy, the spruces' branches root themselves into the soil.

Hikers tread near willows sheltered in the lee of a hill, passing a north-facing and typically late-blooming slope. Willows may harbor the white-crowned sparrow, which nests in the harsh alpine lifezone.

To the east, the rugged Sawtooth rips the skyline. Paint-brush daubs a ridge with flagrant red while far below, Scott Gomer Creek bisects the long valley at Mount Bierstadt's broad base.

Crest the ridge to view Square Top Mountain. Dip a bit before continuing along the fast-fading old road. A saddle area of meadow grasses obscures the roadway, but at the south end a sign points Rosalie Trail #603 to the left along a defined single track, while the hike to Geneva Knob continues straight ahead beyond the signpost. In the distance, Geneva Mountain rises to the south.

Undulating somewhat, the gravely track vaguely etches a turn to the right as Square Top's summit rises. The path then pulls up to a little seasonal pond and bends around toward an outcrop pile. Barely discernible amongst increasingly thick ground vegetation, the track forks right on a saddle, heading out and around to the west of the big outcrop. A pause takes in Square Top, Revenue, and Silver Mountains, leading the eye around to Santa Fe, Geneva, and Landslide Peaks—three thirteeners on the Continental Divide. Defunct Geneva Basin Ski Area carves the foreground.

You can turn around when the trail peters out on the saddle between two outcrops, or loop your way around to the highest rock pile before heading back down the old wagon road. From a likely vantage point, look into Hall Valley far below, and beyond to Red Cone. The long reaches of South Park extend to the south.

Accessibility, grand scenery, myriad mountains, alpine wildflowers, and exhilaratingly rarefied air conspire to make the trek from Guanella Pass to Geneva Knob a tundra-territory winner.

Mount Bierstadt

Trail Rating	strenuous
Trail Length	8.2-mile out-and-back
Elevation	11,669 to 14,065 feet
Amenities	none
Highlights	a spectacular fourteener
Location	Mount Evans Wilderness, Pike National Forest
Directions	From Denver, take I-70 West to Exit 228 at Georgetown and follow signs for Guanella Pass. Park on the east side of the pass, and head toward the willows to access Mount Bierstadt Trail.

One of the luxuries of living in Denver is the unique opportunity to "bag" a fourteener, as the local "peak baggers" say, on a day trip. Not only is Mount Bierstadt's trailhead just an hour's drive from the metro area, but the mountain is one of the easier fourteeners to climb—if anything at this altitude can be called easy. The hike's more apt strenuous rating is due to an elevation gain of about 2,800 feet. Additionally, there is about 40 percent less available oxygen at the summit than at sea level. Rest stops are not optional, they are downright necessary. That goes doubly for adequate water, sun protection, sturdy boots, and outdoor gear in case of changing weather, which can move in with amazing rapidity. Nonetheless, Mount Bierstadt Trail offers a magnificent opportunity for an unforgettable peak experience.

On weekday mornings the parking area looks roomy, but it fills up quickly on summer weekends. When climbing mountains of this magnitude, a very early start cannot be recommended strongly enough. Dawn is not too early, for what begins as a clear summer morning can metamorphose into a violent thunderstorm-filled afternoon. It is best to plan on being back down from the summit around noon. All of the Mount Bierstadt Trail is above tree line, therefore it is completely exposed to lightning and wild weather when storms move in.

Several years ago, the extensive willow carrs that confronted Mount Bierstadt-bound hikers were considered the worst part of the trek. This was changed by an organization called the Colorado Fourteeners Initiative, whose mission includes making the trails that access Colorado's 14,000-foot peaks more hiker-friendly as well as environmentally sensitive. Now, instead of a confusing network of social trails weaving through the wet tangle of willows, a boardwalk keeps boots from trampling myriad paths.

Stand and stare at the towering mountain whose summit is your goal, and take in the Rocky Mountain majesty. Double-check to be sure that you have all the proper gear, then head for the signed gap in the upper parking area and enter Mount Evans Wilderness' 75,400 preserved acres.

Begin descending the Mount Bierstadt Trail towards the once-infamous willows. The Sawtooth, connecting Mount Evans and Mount Bierstadt, sculpts the skyline. A trail coming in from the left leads to an overflow parking area. The sides of the trail are spangled with dozens of wildflower species as the path drifts down, heading for the first of a series of timber boardwalks. Soon you will cross Scott Gomer Creek on boulders.

Willow-girt switchbacks lift the trail past the last of the Engelmann spruces. Atop an age-worn granite outcrop the mountainscape scale grows enormous. As the gradient steepens, a shorter stride will help keep your oxygen intake more even.

A rockfall farther on is a good place to spot the pika, a member of the hare family. Mountain goats also call these heights home. Tundra plants cushion the slopes and the Sawtooth arête commands notice. The trail steadfastly wends up Bierstadt's northwest shoulder. From here, the pitch gets serious, the tread gets rockier, and pauses take on more importance.

The far side of the saddle reveals Frozen Lake below. Angular granitic rock forms the stegosaurus-like backbone you climb to reach the 14,065-foot summit. Choose rocks carefully as you scramble up this last pitch. The stunning 360-degree panorama at the top includes Grays and Torreys Peaks— the only fourteeners in Colorado that straddle the Continental Divide.

The exhilarating accomplishment of having "bagged" Bierstadt is yours if you opt for this ultimate Denver-area day hike.

Hike 53

Pelican Mine Site

Just walking through Silver Plume is an adventure into an era when silver was king. The town was founded in 1870; however, it was the gold rush of 1859 that brought the first inhabitants to the area. Many historic buildings still line the unpaved streets. The stone jail was constructed in 1874 and was used up until 1915. The mammoth—for the size of today's town—1894 brick schoolhouse now houses a museum. Tailing piles from rich mines with names such as Dives, Cherokee, Pelican, Snowdrift, and The 7:30 pock the steep slopes funneling into town. Developing a top-notch mine here confirmed the saying, "It takes a gold mine to make a silver mine."

Park along Silver Plume's Main Street, where your vehicle will not interfere with businesses or residences. The high country stream valley here acts as a funnel for summer afternoon thunderstorms, usually brief but terrific.

To begin the Pelican Mine hike, walk to Silver Street and head north up the hill, passing colorful homes. Surrounded by small aspens, the end of the short street is marked with a sign: The 7:30 Mine Road Recreational Trail. Head right here, within sight of an aged wooden tipple off to the left. This reminder of man's quest for valuable minerals anchors enormous tailings flowing down the mountainside.

Trail Rating	easy to moderate
Trail Length	1-mile out-and-back
Elevation	9,200 to 9,400 feet
Amenities	none
Highlights	old mine site, historic mining town
Location	Silver Plume
Directions	From Denver, take I-70 West to Exit 226 for Silver Plume. Go north, and park along Main Street near where it intersects with Silver Street.

Aiming east along an easy grade takes you above the roofs of Silver Plume to a turn where the road reverses direction and heads west. An 1870s toll gate levied stiff fares here, but for miners this might have been the hopeful "road to riches."

With only quaking aspens for company, embark on a long steady pull up the rocky roadway. Pelican Flats, a level stretch of tailings, is your reward. Here, the feuding Dives and Pelican Mines both claimed the rich silver vein running through a pair of 12,000-foot mountains. Look up slide-prone Cherokee Gulch, marked today by an old boiler. Silver miners, whose lives were already tenuous, suffered more suspense when gunshots culminated in a murder in 1875. The feuding mine owners finally came up with a solution; the two mines merged.

But Cherokee Gulch remained a dangerous place for miners. In the winter of 1899, an avalanche took the lives of 10 Italian mine workers. A granite marker in the Silver Plume cemetery stands in their honor.

Old tracks—remnants of an aerial tram—poke out of the mine tailings. Rusted ore cars litter the slope on the bottom side of the mine flats. The Clear Creek Valley slumbers below, dreaming of the hustle and bustle that once enlivened Silver Plume. Across the way, things are kept lively by the steam engine's whistle as the train winds its way along the Georgetown Loop Railway.

Hiking along the wagon road to easily accessed Pelican Mine is a fine way to visit the bygone era of silver mining's heyday, when avarice and avalanche kept life interesting. A walk through Silver Plume, replete with 19th-century buildings, is a way to further delve into Colorado history.

Argentine Central Railroad Grade

Trail Rating	easy
Trail Length	2.8-mile out-and-back
Elevation	9,250 to 9,650 feet
Amenities	none
Highlights	Georgetown Loop locomotive whistle, mine tipples
Location	Silver Plume
Directions	From Denver, take I-70 West to Exit 226 for Silver Plume. Go under the interstate, and turn right onto the frontage road. Proceed 0.4 mile to the trailhead and parking on the right, just east of a private gate.

In 1906, the Argentine Central Railroad cut a grade across Leavenworth Mountain but discontinued service in 1918. Where narrow-gauge rails once carried ore and later tourists, gentle grades make for a shady saunter above the Clear Creek Valley and the quaint 1870s town of Silver Plume. At the trail's far end, just beyond the second mine tipple, the Georgetown Loop tracks coil below. If the hiker is so inclined, the trail also accesses Pavilion Point for a total of 4 miles round-trip.

Parking is very limited where the trail begins. Watch for summer afternoon thunderstorm activity, and always use caution when exploring areas that have seen mining activity.

South of the small parking area, a roadway angles up to the east. This is the Argentine Central Railroad Grade—your trail for this hike. The gentle gradient, shaded by aspens' shimmering leaves, is wide enough for companionable hiking.

Mixed conifers join the aspens and lead the way up to a vista. Silver Plume, anchored by its big 1894 brick schoolhouse, basks below. From a rocky path to a sandy one, the trail maintains its angle, reaching a causeway that once carried the train to various mines.

From summer green to autumn gold, the season and the moisture levels dictate aspen color. The mass of these smooth-barked trees is affected by moisture too, and their girth increases as the trail approaches an area inhabited by water-loving frothy horsetails and willows. Perhaps you will hear the nostalgic whistle of the Georgetown Loop train as it chuffs up the grade toward Silver Plume, belching black smoke and lonesome locomotive calls.

Steeply sloped tailings lead toward a small unexpected pool, dark as a mine tunnel. Farther on, the rail bed narrows to singletrack for a brief section before resuming its narrow-gauge breadth.

Draw up to an ore tipple leaning into its aging timbers—remember that its stability is compromised more each year. Clinging to the contours of Leavenworth Mountain's north face, the path levels for a moment as it heads toward the second wooden tipple, into which an iron pipe fed ore. Though in slightly better repair than the first, this picturesquely deteriorating feature, weathered into rich golds and browns, is still of uncertain stability. Nonetheless, these relics of a bygone era represent the tumultuous times of the mining era, when digging fortune from steep mountainsides was a rough way of life.

The second tipple is the turnaround point for this description. For those pressing on to Pavilion Point, look for a west-angling switchback just before the second tipple. From here, begin a forest slog, via two very long railroad grade switchbacks, up to Pavilion Point. Only a crudely built chimney that once warmed a dancehall remains.

This shady trail up a historic railroad grade makes a fine short hike into the mining past of the Clear Creek Valley.

Herman Gulch

The trek to the splendid natural gardens of Herman Gulch accelerates the heart rate, especially at the start and on the final pitch to Herman Lake, at 11,900 feet. However, the bountiful wildflower displays and mountain-girt vistas are worth every aerobic step. If a trail's worth can be judged by the number of cars in its parking area, Herman Gulch must be a gem. Although Exit 218 is unnamed, lots of hikers know this is a special trail.

Parking is in a large area that fills quickly. Arrive early in order to beat the crowds and complete the hike before afternoon thunderstorms roll in.

The trail begins through forest on a level path of crusher-fines. Soon after the minced gravel peters out, the route divides. Herman Gulch Trail heads left while Watrous Gulch Trail veers to the right. This junction initiates a steady incline on a wide trail that ends, 1,500 vertical feet later, at Herman Lake. The initial ascent is taxing but not overly long, and the grade finally moderates as the sound of whitewater reports off to the left.

Willows flank the now-level trail. After a tiny rivulet channeled by logs runs across it, the track passes a grassy area before entering forest. Continuing in deep shade, the path passes a spring on the right where moisture-loving wildflowers such as late-summer-blooming gentian flourish.

Trail Rating	moderate to strenuous
Trail Length	6.8-mile out-and-back
Elevation	10,400 to 11,900 feet
Amenities	restrooms
Highlights	fabulous mountainscapes, alpine lake, bountiful columbine in June
Location	Arapaho National Forest
Directions	From Denver, take I-70 West to Exit 218. Turn right and into the parking area.

Up the trail, another streamlet comes into view as evergreens give way to open skies. The rugged face of 13,553-foot Pettingell Peak lies ahead. Wildflowers fill the meadows, and, typically in mid-June, an extravaganza of blue columbine enchants hikers. Although many spots in Colorado boast goodly amounts of the state's stunning flower, the display in Herman Gulch is one of the best. Its fame as such sometimes results in unintentional trampling of the columbine clumps. A floral treasury such as this warrants sensitive viewing, keeping the glorious display intact for future visitors.

A hefty split-log bridge is followed by roots and rocky trail requiring careful boot placement. Soon, switchbacks take the hiker to peak-ringed views that call for appreciation and pause. Myriad wildflowers divert attention as the route grows rougher underfoot and the track heaves up a final pitch.

At last the pathway levels out, and gravelly soil makes walking easier. Krummholz patches of stunted Engelmann spruce and stands of willow accent the mountainscape. On the right, a small pond serves as a harbinger of the objective of this hike—you're almost there.

Set in a mountain-girt bowl, Herman Lake, at 11,900 feet, has lots of boulders on which rest and dine. Like fine Chinese jade, the lake waters are a surprising celadon green. A crystalline creek just west of the lake is lined with many pretty flowers.

Herman Gulch is one of nature's enchanting surprises. It is a great place to experience regal Rocky Mountain scenery, wildflower gardens, and, of course, exhilarating hiking.

Mount Sniktau

Many people enjoy the regal panorama afforded them as they drive to the top of nearly 12,000-foot Loveland Pass. Others stretch their legs and lungs by hiking either east, toward 13,235-foot Mount Sniktau, or west, toward Loveland Ski Area. In late June and early July, the tundra is in gemlike bloom. Wherever one looks, Rocky Mountain majesty is evident.

The first mile of the Mount Sniktau Trail, covered in this description, makes no bones about up. It rises over 500 vertical feet in that mile, which, with one-third less oxygen than one enjoys at sea level, can make breathing rather challenging.

Parking on fine-weather weekends gets competitive despite the large pullout at the pass. An early start helps avoid both the competition and, even more importantly, powerful lightning storms on summer afternoons. This trail is above tree line, making hikers the highest objects on the exposed slopes. It is foolhardy to attempt this route when storms are approaching. Wind is a common companion at this lofty elevation as well, and it can create a substantial chill factor—so layer up.

Mount Sniktau Trail leaves the pullout at the prominent sign for 11,990-foot Loveland Pass and the Continental Divide. The trail forks immediately, but both "tines" rejoin shortly. The right or lower trail is a less strenuous and perhaps more scenic way to begin your hike, for it is more sheltered and has more wildflowers. Yellows are represented by alpine wall-flower and several species of cinquefoil—brassy alpine avens are the most common here. Sky pilot, purple fringe, and daisylike fleabanes compose the purples. Take a moment to examine the sides of the trail for a floristic appreciation of nature's perseverance.

Trail Rating	strenuous
Trail Length	2-mile out-and-back
Elevation	11,990 to 12,500 feet
Amenities	none
Highlights	glorious mountain vistas, tundra flowers
Location	Arapaho National Forest
Directions	From Denver, take I-70 West to Exit 216 for Loveland Pass (US 6). Proceed to the pass, and park in the pullout on the left or east side of the highway.

The trails converge shortly and the incline begins seriously, tackling the first knoll straight on...and up. Taking the angle of ascent slowly helps hikers adjust to the fact that there is less oxygen up here. In this rarefied atmosphere, it seems incredible that small butterflies, some designed like stained-glass windows in ambers and golds, brave the elements to pollinate and gather nectar.

Early summer is a good time to watch insects flit to the tiny floral gems that bloom on the harsh tundra. Within a mere 6–8 weeks, wildflowers must emerge, bud and bloom, and then wait for a pollinator in order to set seed and propagate their species.

The trail crests the knoll and leads onto a saddle—a great place to catch your breath. Take in the fabulous peripheral view that practically begs for you to turn all the way around, so as not to miss the memorable mountainscape.

Another knoll challenges you to continue up, where you'll discover cushions, buns, and mats of enchanting seasonal flowers. Take a moment to explore the lure of some of the flowers by assuming the belly-down, beginning-botanist position. You will be delighted with such perfumed treats as sky-blue alpine forget-me-not, pale starry phlox, and the various tundra clovers.

By the third knoll, the sky will seem higher and wider, and your breathing will be faster and greedier. Countless ranges skewer the skyline, manifesting the fact that Colorado is the highest state overall. From here, the Rockies seem like mid-continent tsunami waves in stone. The trail brings you up to a little rock garden before ascending to a cairned junction with another path that leads southeast along the Continental Divide. This makes a good turnaround point if lofty Mount Sniktau, another steep mile ahead, is not your goal.

A start at Loveland Pass' 12,000-foot trailhead enables hikers to view tundra wildflowers within moments. Add to those petite petals the astounding panorama of peaks and valleys, and you may think you have discovered the place where wonder comes to refresh itself. Feel free to do the same.

Hike 57

Loveland Pass West

Trail Rating	moderate to strenuous
Trail Length	2.6-mile out-and-back
Elevation	11,990 to 12,479 feet
Amenities	none
Highlights	stunning views, alpine wildflowers
Location	Arapaho National Forest
Directions	From Denver, take I-70 West to Exit 216 for Loveland Pass (US 6). Continue to the pass and park at the pullout. Cross the highway to access the West Ridge Trail.

Just an hour west of Denver, 11,990-foot Loveland Pass sits astride the Continental Divide. This is tundra country—with a compass-full of fabulous views and alpine wildflower gems above tree line. Loveland Pass' West Ridge Trail follows the Continental Divide for a good portion of its length. While much of the west "bowl" can be snowbound well into summer, the ridge itself may be hikeable fairly early in the season.

Plenty of parking is available on the pass at the gravel pullout on the east side of US 6. Unpredictable weather such as high winds and wild sudden thunderstorms makes preparedness crucial. At 12,000 feet, very cold temperatures, hail, and snow can hit unexpectedly, even in the summer.

From the starting point on the west side of US 6, a graveled path leads levelly, passing a sign conveying the importance of staying on established trails to protect the fragile, slow-to-heal tundra. A stone-walled overlook, with I-70 traffic whizzing far below, gives visitors a clear view of the west bowl and Loveland Ski Area. The West Ridge Trail continues past the wall in a southerly direction.

A gap revealing the south side of the pass takes the track up on angular rocks. Tight mats, buns, and cushions of vegetation, naturally engineered for success in a harsh habitat, cling to the edges of the rocks. Spruce krummholz (German for crooked wood) blocks the harsh elements with wind-breaking boughs that hug the earth, often rooting into it.

Stay on the apex of the ridge. Knee-high willows lead the way into an area where gravelly soil precedes a steeper climb. Rising on a rocky path, the trail eases a bit, and lower willows shelter wildflowers on either side. Resuming its ascent along the ridge's backbone, the trail is flanked by sheets of creamy-white mountain dyrad—a favorite food of ptarmigan. The track levels, passing a rocky space where pikas, of the ancient order of rabbits and hares, might be seen (or at least heard).

At a break in the ridge, the view expands as you continue along the trail. Encounter hummocky grasses when the trail begins descending toward the base of a rockfall. Here, the hand-span-wide cushions of bright pink moss campion may be up to a century old. Passing briefly between sheltering banks, the track drops to a moist area with late-blooming wildflowers.

The trail rises to a substantial rock cairn at 12,414 feet, pointing west to distant 14,005-foot Mount of the Holy Cross. Another fourteener, Quandary Peak anchors the south end of the Tenmile Range, home to Breckenridge Ski Area. Keystone's winter playground dominates the foreground.

The trail turns north now to follow the Continental Divide. Continue to another small bowl, and look ahead to 13,553-foot Pettingell Peak and 13,195-foot Hagar Mountain, forming part of the divide. Follow the cairns. The way is level until an initial pitch brings it up to a spa-sized ring of rocks. Another pitch brings the hiker up a 360-degree panorama. The trail drops some, then evens out as it passes through a patch of spruce krummholz and willow. The last climb, best done around to the left and up through jumbled rock, arrives at a stone wind shelter with an unsurpassed view.

The open tundra of Loveland Pass offers a convenient window on the world of flowering gems. Stunning vistas of numerous proud Colorado peaks inspire awe.

Denver Foothills

The foothills stretching from just west of Denver to the charming town of Evergreen are perfect for early season hiking. When higher regions are still winter-weary, this area begins to blossom with signs of spring. Wildflowers abound and scenery astounds here, and most of the hikes in this area are just a few paces from Denver's doorstep.

From the ruddy sandstone formations found at Red Rocks and Matthews/Winters Parks to the cool green meadows and ponderosa pine forests at Lair o' the Bear, Elk Meadows, and Alderfer/Three Sisters, this region's open space covers a splendid array of territory that supports a diversity of wildlife and delights adventurers. Some of Jefferson County Open Space's most precious gems lie in this stretch of countryside between the high country and the Great Plains, and you'll get splendid views of both from many of the convenient trails in this region.

The snow-covered
Mount Evans
massif captures
the skyline.

Contents

Denver Foothills
Hikes 58 – 74

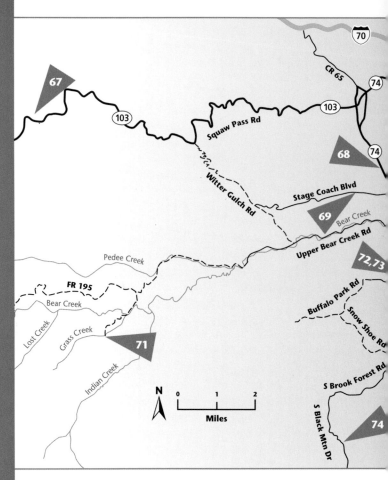

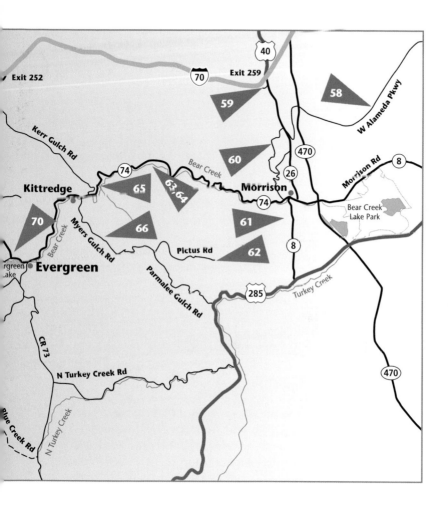

Hayden/Green Mountain Loop

Green Mountain rises like a gentle island in a sea of civilization—an island that is wildflower-happy, especially from late May to late June. While Green Mountain is long on floral color it is short on shade, making early morning or evening hikes ideal. From the top, there is a 360-degree view of Denver, the Dakota Hogback, and several fourteeners that lift the skyline above the foothills of the Front Range.

Sandwiched between creeping suburbia and the high-speed slab of C-470, the rounded body of Green Mountain ranges in elevation from 6,000 feet to 6,800 feet. A number of trails network this open space, including the Hayden/Green Mountain Loop described here. Be aware that rattlesnakes and bull snakes, similar in appearance, call this mountain home. Harmless bull snakes have been known to shake their tails, emulating their venomous rattler cousins. This behavior causes the fangless imitator serious people-trouble.

The large parking area, shared by mountain bikers, is marked by a sign indicating the beginning of the Hayden and Green Mountain Trails. Pick up a handy trail map, and remember that summer afternoon thunderstorms may dampen your spirited hike.

The Hayden Trail leaves from the far end of the parking area and climbs an old jeep road, passing wildflower studded banks. Pause now and then to catch the views of the cityscapes that fan out eastward in a half circle. Contrast the wide-open land on which you stand and the sea of roofs and ribbons of asphalt that radiate into metro Denver. This juxtaposition brings an appreciation for the concept of open space, particularly considering Green Mountain's valuable real estate.

The trail rises quickly toward a radio tower. Farther on, as the trail crests, a short spur on the left presents a mountain view that arcs from south to northwest and includes fourteeners Pikes Peak, Mount Evans, Grays and Torreys Peaks, and Longs Peak.

Continuing north a bit, a well-defined trail angles sharply left and back, aiming for Mount Evans on the western skyline. The downhill leg of the loop begins at this junction and heads through a wealth of wildflowers.

The next trail portion features Pikes Peak straight ahead in the distant south. Waving grasses accompany the leisurely descending route. Farther down the track, small ravines, thick with chokecherry and hawthorn, punctuate the dry slopes. Following the trail map, wind down in a southerly direction, then bear east and finally north up a short incline, paralleling Alameda Parkway back to the parking area.

The city of Lakewood has done itself proud by preserving a whole mountain for the hiker, biker, equestrian, and wildflower enthusiast. Discover many wildflower species during the bloom season, and enjoy the sweeping views Green Mountain offers year-round. A very close-in hike, Hayden/Green Mountain Trail is a quick and gratifying escape.

Trail Rating	moderate
Trail Length	3-mile loop
Elevation	6,080 to 6,770 feet
Amenities	restrooms
Highlights	Mount Evans and city views, wildflowers
Location	Lakewood Regional Parks, Hayden/Green Mountain Park
Directions	From central Denver, take US 6 West and then exit at Union Boulevard. Take Union south for about 1 mile, turn right onto West Alameda Parkway, and proceed for just under 2 miles to the Hayden/Green Mountain Trailhead on the right.

Red Rocks/Morrison Slide Loop

Trail Rating	easy to moderate
Trail Length	4.2-mile balloon loop
Elevation	6,200 to 6,730 feet
Amenities	restrooms, picnic tables
Highlights	views, red sandstone formations, wildflowers
Location	Matthews/Winters Park, Jefferson County Open Space
Directions	From Denver, head west on I-70 to Exit 259. Go south under the highway and look for Matthews/Winters Park shortly on the right.

Convenient to the Denver metro area, Red Rocks/Morrison Slide Trail circles 4 miles, passing the historic 1859 Mt. Vernon town site. The nascent town became instantly popular because citizens who moved there received free lots. Except for a couple of grave markers, the town has nearly vanished. Early season hikers will find this 4.2-mile loop a good one for wildflowers.

Hikers, mountain bikers, and picnickers share the busy parking lot at the trailhead, which often fills on summer weekends. An early start might help secure a parking space and avoid afternoon thunderstorms.

Head down to little Mt. Vernon Creek, cross the footbridge, and travel straight ahead and up to where the trail curves south. Arrive at a split-rail triangle where the short spur to the Mt. Vernon graveyard heads west. Continue south on Red Rocks Trail, observing a nice array of wildflowers before dipping briefly into a small brush-choked ravine.

Following land contours, the undulating track drifts into an arroyo shaded by box elder trees. Under a lone Douglas fir, a seasonal trickle shines. Passing outcrops, rise slightly before cautiously S-curving down a loose segment toward the small creek. Rocky Mountain maple and chokecherry shrubs line the trail as it ascends a switchback. When you reach the trail junction, head up and to the right on the Morrison Slide Trail.

Pause on the ascent and take a moment to study the Dakota Hogback ridge to the east—a locally renowned repository for dinosaur-era evidence. Another switchback angles into juniper, and the steadily climbing trail enters a section of tumbled, red sandstone boulders.

The route zigzags up on rocky footing and bisects an area of big rocks that harbor boulder raspberry shrubs. At last, the ascent ends on a flat bench, and a rest stop on the escarpment's leading edge offers a far-reaching panorama with Green Mountain in the foreground. Among the lichen-encrusted rocks, wildflowers add a touch of color.

Aim toward the bench's far side and drop via rugged switchbacks. Junipers stud the landscape clear to Red Rocks Amphitheatre to the south. Watch your footing on the uneven path as it quickly descends.

The loop continues straight ahead at a junction and heads up a short incline. Farther on, as the route heads north, patches of glossy poison ivy hug the track. Heed the warning: "leaves of three, leave them be..."

The track cruises northwest, now traveling along the escarpment's ragged foot. Once you reach the creek drainage, you've completed the trail's balloon portion—only the string remains. Stay left at the triangle of rail fence, and you'll soon reach clear Mt. Vernon Creek and the trailhead again.

A fine close-in hike in the foothills life zone, right off I-70, Red Rocks/ Morrison Slide Loop is an ideal way to start off the hiking season. Lace up your boots, stride out for some heart-strengthening exercise, and, oh yes...don't forget to lose yourself in the beauty of a wildflower.

Trading Post Loop

Famous for world-class entertainment, Red Rocks Amphitheatre, completed in 1941, is a spectacular outdoor venue reminiscent of an ancient Roman coliseum. This unique venue, formed and surrounded by the monumental red sandstone monoliths of Red Rocks Park, is a special destination.

Trading Post Trail offers a 1.4-mile loop that is surrounded by these masterfully eroded works of nature. Hikers are introduced to the Fountain Formation, which gives the park its stature and the theatre its unique atmosphere. Be sure to check out the trading post, featuring a great selection of outdoor books—especially choice Colorado titles. The snack bar's outdoor balcony embraces an amazing red-rock view. The park's roads also offer stunning views, but plans for a short scenic drive can be hampered when an entertainment event is going on.

Park at the Red Rocks Trading Post, so your vehicle will be convenient to the trailhead. And don't forget to keep a weather eye out for building thunderstorms on summer afternoons.

Begin on the southeast end of the paved parking lot alongside the trading post. Here, a map is posted with the major formations named, including nearby Picnic Rock and Nine Parks Rock. A few steps down and a turn to the left take the trail past rock walls and native shrubs such as wild plum and

Trail Rating	easy
Trail Length	1.4-mile loop
Elevation	6,200 to 6,400 feet
Amenities	restrooms, trading post
Highlights	huge sandstone formations, theatre in the rocks, views
Location	Red Rocks Park, Denver Mountain Parks
Directions	From C-470 on the west side of Denver, take the Morrison/ CO 74 exit. Head west thru town on CO 74 and turn right onto Red Rocks Drive. Continue 1.1 miles and turn left, keeping an eye out for the trailhead on the right (east) side of the Red Rocks Trading Post.

three-leaf sumac. Cacti leads the descending path onto a bedrock sector as you skirt an arroyo filled with small trees—don't walk too close to the edge here.

As the angle steepens, hikers head down to stone stairs that precede and follow a road crossing. The trail then eases, passing through sloping grassy meadows featuring native big bluestem, or turkeyfoot grass.

Within sight of the Dakota Hogback formation, the route turns from south to west and crosses an arroyo via a sturdy footbridge. Punctuated by jutting red sandstone hoodoos and shapely Frog Rock, the trail curves to arrive at a road crossing.

The track rises steadily, passing massive and magnificent layered sculptures of 300-million-year-old sandstone. The next section winds gently up an old roadbed, becoming more personal as it weaves between formations and wild plum thickets. A grassy bowl, surrounded by more of that grandly eroded rock, leads up to a wall. Above, bedding layers tower like gargantuan waves that froze before breaking.

The trail heads up a long series of rock steps, shaded by overarching boughs, in close proximity to a high Fountain Formation wall. When you arrive at a road, you have two options. You can continue on the narrow footpath on the right side of the road for a quick return to Red Rocks Trading Post, or you can cross the road and ascend the steep walkway up to amazing Red Rocks Amphitheatre—an experience that shouldn't be missed. The view of the Denver cityscape and the Great Plains beyond is memorable, as is the vast open-air theatre cradled between the 400-foot monoliths of Ship Rock and Creation Rock.

Right next door to Denver, in the foothills, Red Rocks Park presents an opportunity to explore monolithic grandeur on a unique loop that can include the fabulous amphitheatre.

Turkey Trot/Castle Loop

Trail Rating	moderate
Trail Length	3-mile loop
Elevation	6,200 to 6,800 feet
Amenities	restrooms, picnic sites
Highlights	cityscape and Red Rocks Park views
Location	Mount Falcon Park, Jefferson County Open Space/Morrison
Directions	From C-470 on the west side of Denver, take the Morrison/ CO 74 exit. Head west through town on CO 74 and turn left onto CO 8. Turn right on Forest Avenue, right again onto Vine Avenue, and proceed to the Mount Falcon East parking area and trailhead.

With a name like Turkey Trot, you might think big dark fowls frequent this route on the east side of Mount Falcon. Even if you don't spot wild turkeys, trekking Turkey Trot's hiker-only trail is a great way to explore some foothills-zone habitat including grassland, shrubland, and forest. The remainder of the loop is on multi-use Castle Trail. The eastern reaches of 2,100-plus-acre Mount Falcon Park are administered by the town of Morrison and the rest is under the jurisdiction of Jefferson County Open Space. Views are grand from every level.

Specifically designated for hikers, Turkey Trot's 1.7 miles ease to a dip, then switchback up 600 vertical feet. If you choose not to complete the loop on the biker-shared Castle Trail, described in this entry, retrace Turkey Trot for an out-and-back hike of 3.4 miles.

The large Mount Falcon East parking lot is shared by mountain bikers and can get crowded. An early-morning or weekday hike is bound to be the more pleasant experience. Keep in mind that thunderstorms often form on summer afternoons.

From the west edge of the parking lot, pass through a rail fence and enjoy seasonal wildflowers. Arrive at a fork where hiker-only Turkey Trot Trail takes off to the right. A few junipers and a pond view guide the way into a ravine that precedes an arroyo. Begin an ascent assisted by switchbacks. The gradient makes for some aerobic exercise as the rocky trail passes through shrubland featuring mountain mahogany bushes.

Pause and look to the east over the stegosaurus-like backbone of the Dakota Hogback, and espy Denver's downtown core surrounded by a welter of suburbia. Watch for bits of poison ivy here and there—leaves of three, leave them be. Sandstone has been underfoot so far, but now glittering metamorphic rock dominates the trail. Look to the northwest for a great view of the slanted Fountain Formation at Red Rocks Amphitheatre.

A resolute pine marks a brief level sector before Turkey Trot Trail becomes rocky and rising again. Junipers offer pools of shade in which you can pause to view millions of years of geologic history. Look for the Dakota Hogback in front of Green Mountain, the buff-colored Lyons Formation, and the iron-oxide stained Fountain Formation. Beside the track ahead you'll notice pink igneous rock—Pikes Peak granite.

A saddle reveals a ravine populated with cottonwoods and scrub oak, as the track levels, even dips for a moment, before traversing up to a 180-degree vista. Not to be outdone, high peaks claim the next view.

The trail heads into the ponderosa pine belt, then undulates along on the north face of Mount Falcon. Stately Douglas firs spire skyward and vegetation thickens as the trail moves into a wilder but assuasive landscape, contrasting the harsh dry ascent you've just bested.

The trail travels farther on forested slopes, swinging in and out of shallow ravines before a switchback raises it to a junction. Pause for a glimpse of the far mountains.

A left turn onto Castle Trail sends hikers down an uneven road-wide trail in the company of mountain bikers. The trail switchbacks quickly down through a fully vegetated ravine before returning to the parking area.

Awesome views of plains, cityscapes, distant peaks, and ancient rock formations are your reward for tackling Mount Falcon's Turkey Trot and Castle Trails.

Castle/Tower/Meadow Loop

Covering more than 2,100 acres with 11 miles of trails, Mount Falcon Open Space offers a nice selection of hikes from which to choose. Most share a common trailhead at the west parking area. Be sure to visit the stone ruins of John Walker's home, as well as the site on which he planned to build the Summer White House—a retreat for U.S. presidents. Alas, his impressive home went up in flames in 1918, and the foundation of the Summer White House, visible from the aptly named Walker's Dream Trail, was all that became of his vision.

Parking, shared by picnickers, is at a premium on summer weekends. Come early or late to assure a space, keeping in mind that thunderstorms often brew on warm afternoons.

Big ponderosa pines shade picnic tables where Mount Falcon's broad Castle Trail heads east from the parking lot. A map and a bit of area history front the trail kiosk. The road-wide trail heads off into ponderosa parkland and dips before rising gently into a fire-ravaged area. Granite outcrops overlook flowery spaces here.

The route goes right at a junction where a double-sided bench offers a westward view of 14,265-foot Mount Evans. Continue on toward sturdy Eagle Eye Shelter, which boasts a view clear to the Continental Divide.

From this point, the route rises on peeled log water bars and strikes out onto the Tower Trail. You'll shortly arrive at the old fire tower for which this trail is named. Views to the east include the stone ruins you will encounter later on the loop. The trail continues over a rounded ridge and drops through scrub oak on a south-facing slope. An S-curve leads down into a conifer parkland.

Thinning Douglas fir opens to a wide meadow, and a bench marks the junction where the route joins the Meadow Trail. The path pushes up to a left turn and continues through young Douglas fir and ponderosa pine. A breeze may strum long ponderosa needles with a soothing soughing. Keen-eyed hikers might spot the yellow and black avian with the bright red head: the western tanager. A tiny creeklet, crossed by a bridge, reveals rushes and sedges as the track enjoys a southern exposure.

The trail comes out just before the desecrated remains of Walker's residence. Fireplace stones jut into the sky, filling in the empty spaces where his lovely home once stood. Turn left onto road-wide Castle Trail to complete the loop and return to the parking area. A right turn here will bring you to Walker's Dream Trail and the Summer White House Ruins, adding 1.6 round-trip miles to the route.

Hiking Castle/Tower/Meadow Loop on Mount Falcon is a wonderful way to catch views, learn some local history, and savor a goodly serving of foothills wildflowers. Take a spur-of-the-moment hike on this easy and convenient trail when the desire for exercise and exhilaration calls for a quick escape.

Trail Rating	easy
Trail Length	3.7-mile loop
Elevation	7,700 to 7,850 feet
Amenities	picnic tables, restrooms
Highlights	historic overlook, ruins, wildflowers
Location	Mount Falcon Park, Jefferson County Open Space
Directions	From C-470 on the west side of Denver, take the Morrison/CO 74 exit, and head west through town, and continue for 7.9 miles. Turn left on Myers Gulch Road, proceed 5 miles to Pictus Road, and follow signs to Mount Falcon's west parking area.

Bruin Bluff Loop

Lair o' the Bear nestles in an east-west canyon through which fair-sized Bear Creek flows. State-of-the-art restrooms, handicapped-accessible picnic facilities and fishing spots, hiking trails, and numerous wildflowers make the park an excellent close-in destination. The Bruin Bluff Loop covers several habitats—from riparian areas and rocky outcrops to conifer forests, grassy slopes, and dry scrubland—making this hike a varied adventure.

Parking is generous, but the popularity of Lair o' the Bear makes it a busy place on weekends. Don't forget the possibility of summer afternoon thunderstorms.

Bruin Bluff Trail is accessed by the Brittlefern or Creekside Trails, which carry hikers west to the Dipper Bridge. The sturdy bridge is named for the American dipper, also called the water ouzel. This slate-colored bird likes to stroll underwater for its dinner. It begins its dipping motion by bending at the ankle in a quick curtsey before plunging into the little stream.

After passing over Dipper Bridge the route turns right, toward a bench on the left. Head west to climb a rocky slope that is dotted with mountain mahogany shrubs.

The trail continues on the south side of Bear Creek Canyon, leveling out along a north-facing exposure. Conifers appear, joined by early season blooms such as downy, soft-purple pasqueflowers by the hundreds, perhaps thousands. Benches are strategically placed along the trail.

Near the high point of the trail (which never goes very high) is a rugged outcrop—an example of Mother Nature's xeric rock-gardening efforts. The path switchbacks down from this rock formation. Stay right

Trail Rating	easy
Trail Length	2-mile loop
Elevation	6,520 to 6,780 feet
Amenities	restrooms, picnic sites, water pump
Highlights	views of Bear Creek
Location	Lair o' the Bear, Jefferson County Open Space
Directions	From C-470 on the west side of Denver, take the Morrison/CO 74 exit. Head west through town for 5.4 miles to Lair o' the Bear Open Space Park.

on Bruin Bluff Trail as the track levels and passes a junction with Castor Cutoff Trail. In the cool shade of a noble ponderosa, an inviting bench with a pleasant view beckons.

As the route approaches Bear Creek again, head left under cottonwoods, box elders, and willows. Reach a streamside bench on the right next to Ouzel Bridge. Once over the bridge, aim left past some picnic sites and yet another bench. The restrooms mark the return route to the parking area, and a water pump offers cool refreshment along the way. A picnic under huge trees makes a suitable finish for this nature-filled hike.

A slope on the park's east end is worth a visit in the autumn. The hillside is blanketed with smooth or scarlet sumac, which turns a brilliant red at summer's end. The extent of the color show depends on how much sumac pruning the resident mule deer population has done during the growing season. It is also interesting to note that the sumac's blunt stems sometimes display the same velvety appearance as a buck's antlers during the summer growing season.

Lair o' the Bear is a park for all seasons. A wide variety of wildflowers, an autumn display of blazing red sumac, and an inviting creek make this close-in open space an excellent destination.

Creekside/Castle Loop

Bear Creek provides the music, trees provide the shade, and your feet provide the transportation—a winning combination that makes the stroll along Creekside Trail a pleasure. This level hike through riparian habitat offers an across-the-creek peek at a unique residence casually called "the castle." The unusual sight intrigues visitors of all ages. This trail also includes a 0.2-mile nature bypass along the riverbank.

Generous parking is shared by picnickers, hikers, and anglers. Summer afternoons often spawn thunderstorms, so be alert.

Stop at the trail kiosk for a route map before setting off on your hike. By going south—straight ahead toward Bear Creek—you will encounter Creekside Trail. A turn to the right leads you upstream along a shaded path next to the water. Be aware that an occasional patch of poison ivy might appear trailside. In June, heavy pink racemes of New Mexican locust trees perfume the air.

Trail Rating	easy
Trail Length	3-mile out-and-back with nature loop
Elevation	6,520 feet
Amenities	restrooms, picnic sites, water pump
Highlights	lively creek, autumn color, "castle"
Location	Lair o' the Bear, Jefferson County Open Space
Directions	From C-470 on the west side of Denver, take the Morrison/ CO 74 exit. Head west through town and continue for 5.4 miles to Lair o' the Bear Open Space Park.

Birdsong abounds in the narrowleaf cottonwood trees overhead as Creek-side Trail turns to the left. Pass a bench and bridge and continue straight ahead. An open area flanked by lanky willows reveals a small nature trail that hugs the water. This left-turn diversion rejoins the main trail shortly, and is a great place for kids to get cozy with Mother Nature's lush side. Observe her viny profusion of wild hops and western clematis twining up every tree and shrub in sight.

Back on the main trail, take a left to continue west toward a burly half-log bench. Step over a little tributary making its way to Bear Creek. Farther on, a sturdy bridge brings hikers to the south bank of the stream.

A private property sign on the right readies you for an unusual sight. Mixed woods reveal glimpses of a nearly hidden stone castle. The wooden waterwheel you see once generated electricity for the unique residence. This is the secret of Creekside/Castle Trail—an imaginative hideaway of fairytale proportions, down to its crenellated ramparts. Continue along to a less obstructed view of the structure before turning to retrace your steps. You can extend the hike by tearing your fanciful imagination from the castle and turning back to the footpath on your side of the creek.

Note a rock face hung with vegetation such as bracted alumroot and waxflower shrubs. The latter species has been in existence some 40 million years and sports perfect porcelain-like blooms. Wild raspberry abounds here, too.

Shade gives way to open skies as you head toward Lair o' the Bear's west margin. As it approaches the boundary sign, a trail careens off a slope to the south, and so do the mountain bikers descending it. This bit of trail is part of a network that ties this open space to Corwina, O'Fallon, and Pence Parks. Picnic-perfect sites, often sheltered by huge trees, invite a well-earned meal at the hike's end.

For a saunter alongside bright water speckled by leap-frog shade, try Creekside/Castle Trail at Lair o' the Bear. An otherworldly castle highlights this hike.

Corwina to Panorama Point

Trail Rating	easy to moderate
Trail Length	3-mile out-and-back
Elevation	6,800 to 7,300 feet
Amenities	restroom, picnic sites
Highlights	view, tiny stream
Location	Corwina, Denver Mountain Parks
Directions	From C-470 on the west side of Denver, take the Morrison/CO 74 exit. Head west through town, and continue for 8 miles to milepost 11, then take the first left, over a bridge, to the trailhead and parking area.

Several outdoor-recreation entities have put their hiking and biking heads together and carved trails that connect parks such as Jefferson County's Lair o' the Bear with Denver Mountain Parks' Corwina and O'Fallon. Corwina Park boasts an access trail that is part of this network and used to reach Panorama Point. From that high spot atop an outcrop, hikers are rewarded with views of the commanding Mount Evans massif. The shady trail ascends gently along its first half, but the spur to Panorama Point makes the second half more demanding, attaining an elevation of 500 feet above Bear Creek.

Parking, shared by picnickers, is adequate. Thunderstorms are possible on summer afternoons.

Overshadowed by a looming outcrop overlooking Bear Creek, stone steps flanked by a peeled log fence mark the beginning of Corwina Park's trail to Panorama Point. The narrow path climbs steadily up a shaded ravine, beside a dainty creeklet. Sheltered by conifers such as Colorado blue spruce and Douglas fir, riparian tranquility reigns. A sprinkling of shooting stars tucked into lush vegetation ask for keen observation. Look for these hot-pink flowers where the tiny waterway nurtures emerald grasses, alders, and Rocky Mountain maple. Other early season wildflowers such as snowy meadow anemone may also catch your attention.

Enjoy even footing as the trail leads under big ponderosa pines and arrives at a copse of quaking aspens. You might notice summer-blooming monarda or beebalm. Pulsing like rosy-purple fountains, this member of the mint family is a nectar magnet to which bees and butterflies are pulled.

After a short time, the waterway forms a horseshoe bend among thick willows, announcing the intersection of a trail from adjacent O'Fallon Park. Watch for merging mountain bikers on this blending trail.

Soon after the junction, an oxbow curve changes a southerly heading to a northerly one. About 240 yards from the intersection, a grassy slope should be carefully surveyed for a lesser-used spur trail on the right. This route leads up to Panorama Point. The main trail continues several miles up and over a ridge to drop into Lair o' the Bear Open Space Park.

From this juncture the trail to Panorama Point serpentines up through pines, assisted by an occasional series of steps. Prepare to trek uphill in order to reach the ridge crest.

Follow the ridge to an outcrop where a stunning vista features Mount Evans' 14,265-foot summit. This majestic fourteener is surrounded by its massif companions Mount Goliath and Mount Epaulet. Bask in your accomplishment by taking in this impressive Rocky Mountain Front Range finale at Panorama Point.

From the diminutive streamlet beginning with its early summer shooting stars, to the big-sky view of Mount Evans at the end, the rewards of this hike are as diverse as Colorado itself.

Westridge Loop

This section of O'Fallon Park is a perfect bit of quiet backcountry close to the Denver suburbs. In just 2.5 miles, O'Fallon's Westridge Trail takes the hiker up to a pine-shaded overlook for a gander at 14,265-foot Mount Evans. Descending a ridge through ponderosas, it passes a hidden seasonal creek and a meadow full of wildflowers for a fine outing.

Parking in the pullout area is limited, so arrive early. Thunderstorms might show up on summer afternoons.

An old road accesses O'Fallon Park's Westridge Trail. Ascending quickly to the ridge's saddle, the trail takes a left turn, passing a rounded granite boulder before rising to enter ponderosa pine forest. Steep but brief pitches pull the decomposed granite track to a view of the Mount Evans massif framed by evergreen battalions. At the top of the knoll, hikers might hear birdsong in the early morning hours.

The trail roughens as it rounds to a north slope, coiling down by outcrops to follow a forested ridge. Easygoing now, Westridge Trail turns right

Trail Rating	easy to moderate
Trail Length	2.5-mile loop
Elevation	7,350 to 7,550 feet
Amenities	none
Highlights	Mount Evans view, riparian wildflower habitat
Location	O'Fallon, Denver Mountain Parks
Directions	From C-470 on the west side of Denver, take the Morrison/CO 74 exit. Head west through town, continue for 7.9 miles, and turn left on Myers Gulch Road. Go 1.4 miles to a small parking pullout on the left near a cabled gate barrier.

onto an abandoned roadway and passes grassy slopes on the way to a view to the north with I-70 in the distance.

Young conifers point the way east along a gentle incline to a saddle and vista where the trail heads south. The route descends in the direction of a meadow valley, leaving pine parklands for open slopes. Quaking aspens and willows take over as you approach the hidden stream—a seasonal waterway with overarching plant life.

Bikes are not allowed along this sector of Westridge, where the companionable old roadway parallels the riparian zone above the west bank. Bikers are to be found on the east bank of the stream, on Bear Creek Trail.

On your left, lush vegetation hides whatever water there might be underneath an emerald cloak. Continue south in the dappled shade of dancing aspen leaves. Travel past smooth white trunks until you reach an intersection where hikers share the route with bikers. Turn to the right.

As the road gradually ascends, willows surrounded by deep grasses are perfect backgrounds for colorful wildflowers. Listen for the broad-tailed hummingbird's trilling whir as he climbs into the sky, only to dive earthward at blurring speeds.

Plush grasses leave the willows behind as the track pulls up to curve around the head of a luxurious meadow. Carry on levelly until the route eases up a gradient, returning you to the saddle where the balloon portion of this hike began. Only the short downhill string remains as you head back to the parking pullout.

Westridge Trail at O'Fallon Park is a close-in getaway. A secluded stream valley rewards you with bright wildflowers and birdsong.

Chief Mountain

Trail Rating	moderate to strenuous
Trail Length	3-mile out-and-back
Elevation	10,680 to 11,709 feet
Amenities	none
Highlights	fabulous peak views, tundra flora
Location	Arapaho National Forest
Directions	From Denver, take I-70 West to CO 74 (Exit 252) and head south. Turn right onto Squaw Pass Road (CO 103) and continue for 12.3 miles to an unmarked parking area on the right, just beyond mile marker 19. The trailhead, across the road and up a bit, is marked by a concrete post numbered 290.

On top of 11,709-foot Chief Mountain, panoramas claim every point of the compass. A pirouette of peaks spins around you, including fourteeners Mount Evans, Longs Peak, Grays and Torreys Peaks, and Pikes Peak. Interesting outcrops define the summit itself, and contorted ancient bristlecone pines march downslope. In the latter part of June, tiny tundra treasures bloom, showing off their gemlike colors.

Though the distance is gentle, hiking in the subalpine and alpine zones requires greater effort than hiking in the lowlands. Up here, oxygen levels are about 30 to 35 percent less than at sea level. You'll also gain over a thousand feet in elevation over the course of 1.5 miles. These factors give the hike to Chief Mountain its moderate to strenuous rating, but the rewards for your high-elevation efforts are great.

Parking is on the shoulder of the north side of Squaw Pass Road (CO 103). Note that you will be the highest thing on top of Chief Mountain's barren summit, and "human lightning rod" is a dangerous occupation. Avoid forceful summer afternoon thunderstorms by beginning this hike in the early morning.

Start your ascent on the south side of Squaw Pass Road and quickly rise up the bank to a concrete post marked 290. The longest section of this climb is spent trudging through a subalpine fir and Engelmann spruce forest, but it is accomplished on gentle switchbacks.

An open area, practically paved with flat rock, introduces bristlecone pine. At this hike's halfway point, you are rewarded by views of Grays and Torreys Peaks—the only fourteeners on the Continental Divide. South and North Arapaho Peaks and Mount Audubon in the Indian Peaks Wilderness are extra bonuses. Spruces are stunted and rock is dominant, but a hike in the right season—typically mid-to-late June, and early July in a deep snow-pack year—reveals a varied array of blooming tundra gems.

Feast your color-hungry eyes on such ground-hugging jewels as forget-me-nots in that special Colorado-sky blue; lovely rose-pink fairy primroses; mertensia dressed in deepest matte blue; and the sunshine pigments of the alpine avens, alpine parsley, and goldflower. In the short alpine summer of six to eight weeks, these beautiful little marvels go through their entire reproduction cycle.

The trail travels through a rock garden below the summit jumble, where tundra grasses and flowers dwell between the scattered boulders. Two ragged outcrops look like the finned backs of prehistoric lizards, and the Mount Evans massif lies between them in the distance—a landlocked whale caught in the shallows.

Clamber with care up the picturesque north pile of sparkling granitic confusion to stand on Chief Mountain's 11,709-foot summit, and take in the plains-to-peaks views. A plastic pipe cabled to the rock houses the summit register. Sign in if you like. At the top of Chief Mountain, you are heir to Rocky Mountain majesty.

Painter's Pause/Meadow View/ Founders Loop

Today's hikers, like pioneering homesteaders and cattlemen before them, deem this wide meadow in Jefferson County Open Space a fine place. Oh, to be offered 160-acre tracts in such a lovely area, as was tendered to home-steaders in 1869. Thirteen miles of trail weave through the nearly 1,400 acres of Elk Meadow Park, and 2.5 of them are covered in this description. Painter's Pause, a short section of Meadow View, and a return on Founders complete the balloon loop. Be sure to pick up a trail brochure for an overview of this open space gem.

Parking is generous at this popular trailhead but can be tight on week-ends. Keep an eye out for building thunderheads on summer afternoons.

Start out on a raised bed of crusher-fines, leading to the right for a brief stint on Sleepy "S" Trail. Pass a family of ponderosa pines and drift down to meet Painter's Pause.

A turn to the left sends the string of the balloon loop north, passing a bright green wetlands area smattered with wildflowers. Wide-open spaces lead the eye west to the summit of Bergen Peak, as a boardwalk spans another damp zone. If it weren't for Evergreen Parkway's modern reminder, the vast meadowlands might look as they did well over a century ago.

Trail Rating	easy
Trail Length	2.5-mile balloon loop
Elevation	7,600 to 7,980 feet
Amenities	restrooms
Highlights	vast meadow
Location	Elk Meadow Park, Jefferson County Open Space
Directions	From Denver, take I-70 West to CO 74 (Exit 252), and head south to Elk Meadow Park's Lewis Ridge Road entrance. Turn right and proceed to the parking area and trailhead.

A small barn appears on the right before the junction with Founder's Trail, the path on which this loop will return. For now, stay straight ahead on Painter's Pause. Various birds and blooms perk up the landscape as the route dips a bit and encounters another small wetlands spanned by a raised track.

Rise into the welcome shade of lonesome ponderosa patriarchs. Continue north to view the Squaw Pass Road to Mount Evans. The first stretch of this scenic byway is a good place to spot elk herds, especially when they drift into the far edges of the big meadow, or congregate on the hillside north of the road in their wintering grounds.

The next trail junction sends the loop left for a segment on the Meadow View Trail. Drift gently up as the route turns southerly. Stately ponderosa parkland, underlain by granitic outcrops, sports an inviting bench.

After enjoying the pooled pine shade afforded by the vanilla-scented ponderosa, you'll meet the Founders Trail where the loop makes a turn to the left. A broad hairpin bends the path out into the open meadow again.

A half-circle trail offshoot pulls the hiker to a long curved pair of interestingly finished concrete benches. Here an interpretive sign honors the legacy of Jefferson County Open Space. Guarded by a trio of noble ponderosas, a nearby plaque commemorates those who spearheaded the efforts to preserve the parkland we enjoy today. Soon after, the balloon portion closes, rejoining the Painter's Pause Trail, which leads back to the parking lot.

The gentle and expansive demeanor of this balloon loop encourages hikers, bikers, runners, and saunterers alike to enjoy meadowland virtues and wide-open views.

Meadow View/Elkridge/ Sleepy "S" Loop

Trail Rating	easy
Trail Length	2.6-mile balloon loop
Elevation	7,760 to 8,120 feet
Amenities	restrooms, picnic sites
Highlights	foothills and montane hike
Location	Elk Meadow Park, Jefferson County Open Space
Directions	From Denver, take I-70 West to CO 74 (Exit 252) and head south. Turn right on Stagecoach Boulevard, and proceed for 1.25 miles to the trailhead and parking area on the right.

Located north of Evergreen and south of Bergen Park, Elk Meadow Open Space welcomes hikers to an island refuge of wildlife and wildflowers. The park's nearly 1,400 acres also includes a wildlife preserve where elk can sometimes be seen in impressive numbers. Resonant bugling reams the air during the fall rut as bulls vie for harems. Whether or not you spot the elusive elk, the 2.6-mile Meadow View/Elkridge/Sleepy "S" Loop is worth a trip.

Shared by bikers and picnickers, the parking lot at the Meadow View Trailhead fills quickly on weekends. Come early, or better yet, on a weekday. A gravel path leads to wheelchair-accessible picnic tables and restrooms. Be alert for afternoon thunderstorms in summer.

After a stop at the trail kiosk, bypass picnic sites and continue on the gravel path toward handy restroom facilities. Shaded by big pines, the track rises en route to a junction where the loop leads left on Meadow View Trail. Meadow grasses are accented by bright wildflowers before the trail enters a coniferous forest and the narrowing path penetrates deep shade. Along the way, forest openings encourage aspen and Rocky Mountain maple. Before the track arrives at the first switchback, evergreen mats of kinnikinnick line the way.

A second switchback takes the easing trail by some boulders just before the Bergen Peak turnoff. Continue on Meadow View Trail as it swings east to traverse a southern exposure.

Before long, a junction anchored by a bench takes the loop right, along Elkridge Trail. The track is level at first, then, where mica sparkles underfoot, it descends via switchbacks into ponderosa parkland.

The next intersection turns the loop right onto Sleepy "S" Trail. The track is even now as it heads back in a southwesterly direction, passing a beckoning bench. Before the trail starts rising comfortably through large ponderosas, it passes boulders hosting requisite boulder raspberry shrubs. In spring, just before the path makes its first sleepy "S" curve, a nice stand of wild iris blooms on the left. Another inviting bench soon appears to the left.

Just beyond, the loop rejoins Meadow View Trail where a turn to the left leads you back to the parking area. Fall is a good time to look for elk when you drive north toward I-70; check the park brochure for the locations of wildlife preserves and the Noble Meadow conservation easement.

When the elk are in residence, one way to spot them is to head north on CO 74 along the east boundary of Elk Meadow Open Space, then head west on Squaw Pass Road along the north boundary. Stop and sight across a vast valley meadow (binoculars are immeasurably helpful) to the aspen-edged forest. Sometimes, in winter, the elk congregate west of the fence line on a hillside north of the road to Squaw Pass.

In its 2.6 miles, Meadow View/Elkridge/Sleepy "S" Loop offers a fine hiking experience, and makes for a nice cross-country ski in the wintertime. Little more than 30 minutes from the Denver metro area, this bit of Jefferson County Open Space is popular year-round.

Evergreen Lake Loop

Like a present-day Currier and Ives print, skaters twirl and kids frolic or chase hockey pucks on frozen Evergreen Lake during the winter season. In summer, a leisurely paddle on the dancing waters is a perfect outing, especially since the lake is surrounded by trees, a slice of golf course, wetlands, and a few picturesque structures. Rental boats are available during the summer season. Visitors can encircle the lake via boardwalk, footbridge, natural surface pathways, and steel steps—quite a varied track for a 1-mile loop. And all this is adjacent to the center of old downtown Evergreen.

Weekend parking in the paved lot is competitive, regardless of the season. An occasional glance at the sky on summer afternoons may alert you to a building thunderstorm.

The Lake House is an imposing log structure and the starting point for the 1-mile trail that encircles jewel-like Evergreen Lake.

Starting out from the south side of the Lake House, head lakeside on crusher-fines and note a larger-than-life statue. A vintage boardwalk passes the old sod-roofed boathouse—the original "lake house"—built by the Civilian Conservation Corps in 1932. As you continue in an easterly direction next to the water, look for waterfowl paddling or sunning on Evergreen Lake's sparkling surface. The adjacent banks, accessed by a wide boardwalk, are ideal for fishermen or families.

Arcing gracefully, a metal bridge lifts you over a wildflower-dotted area to continue your walk around the south shore. An angled boardwalk-cum-fishing deck, replete with inviting built-in benches, supports a host of leisure opportunities.

Trail Rating	easy
Trail Length	1-mile loop
Elevation	7,072 to 7,112 feet
Amenities	restrooms in Lake House facility (when open), picnic tables
Highlights	ice skating in winter, boat rental in summer
Location	Evergreen Parks & Recreation; Dedisse Park, Denver Mountain Parks
Directions	From Denver, take I-70 West to CO 74 (Exit 252) and head south. Turn right onto Upper Bear Creek Road and continue for 0.3 mile to the Evergreen Lake entrance on the left.

As it curves toward the north along an outcrop wall, the path skips through ponderosa shade. Prepare to mount a set of gripping steel stairs, and descend on the far side to a footbridge spanning spillway waters. A commanding copy of one of Frederic Remington's renderings of a mountain man on horseback invites a pause. A short bridge nearby takes you into a circular demonstration garden of xeric plants.

The garden path rejoins the main route to cross over the Bear Creek outlet. Ascend stairs to the pathway on the lake's north bank and cruise west. A drop to lake level introduces you to an alder-studded wetlands habitat that harbors water-lovers such as mallards, big blue herons, and black cormorants. Pleasantly level, the trail bends left to another arced bridge, followed by a boardwalk. Bisecting a cattail wetlands beloved by cheerful red-winged blackbirds, the loop now heads back to the parking lots. A stone sculpture of playing children marks the end of the loop.

For a gem of a close-in 1-mile walk, try the Evergreen Lake Loop just west of old downtown Evergreen.

Hike 71

Grass Creek

Upper Bear Creek Road, west of Evergreen, provides a scenic entry for reaching Grass Creek Trail. The trail, located in Mount Evans State Wildlife Area, offers a wonderful strolling stretch along peaceful golden Bear Creek. Early homesteaders must have also valued this tranquility. A stone chimney marks their old dwelling place beside Bear Creek.

The 2.1-mile trail includes a number of elevation gains and losses, making for occasional heart-pounding efforts. This well-managed area is open to fall hunting, and public access is prohibited from January 1 through June 14. (Check with authorities for hunting season periods before setting off.)

Also consider the strong possibility of some summer afternoon thunderstorm activity. Be prepared for them, or, better yet, avoid them altogether with an early hike. Parking at the trailhead is usually adequate.

Spanning an old road serving as trail, a wide metal gate stands at the Grass Creek Trailhead. After passing around the red gate, head up a steady incline where wildflowers dot the golden granite banks. Flanked by small black-scarred quaking aspens, the crest of the hill comes none too soon. Drift down the south side of the hill past flakes of granite and listen for the murmur of running water.

Flowing smoothly in its winding amber bed, Bear Creek announces a long level stretch where Colorado blue spruces spire into the mountain air. Creek-sounds are life-sounds in the water-conscious West.

Off to one side of the roadway, great blocks of granite precede an open meadow area. Prescribed burns took place in this small valley bisected by lovely Bear Creek. Ahead, moisture-loving willows stand guard over a sturdy

Trail Rating	easy to moderate
Trail Length	4.2-mile out-and-back
Elevation	8,700 to 9,400 feet
Amenities	restroom, picnic tables
Highlights	hidden creek in old homestead area, peaks view
Location	Mount Evans Elk Management Area, Mount Evans State Wildlife Area
Directions	From Denver, take I-70 West to CO 74 (Exit 252) and head south. Turn right onto Upper Bear Creek Road and proceed for 6 miles. Take the left fork and follow signs for approximately 3 miles to the well-marked entrance. The trailhead and picnic area are about 1.5 miles down the road.

plank bridge where the trail reluctantly leaves the meandering stream. Bright-winged Aphrodite fritillaries and swallowtail butterflies flutter by.

The bridge over Bear Creek is a good turnaround point for those who don't wish to test their heart rate. View seekers can exercise their lungs and their perseverance by continuing up the trail. After crossing Bear Creek, it is a long, aerobic climb to reach an undulating flat that leads to an emerald blanket all but concealing Grass Creek. Beyond this great meadow is Mount Evans' snowy folds.

Continuing up the wide forest-flanked road brings hikers up to sparse aspen. The steady pull ascends to a trio of craggy granite rocks on the right. These outcrops frame a single contorted pine and frame a keyhole glimpse of Mount Evans. The track enters an area of big ponderosa pines.

Drift down through birdsong and soughing pines to reach a small sign for Grass Creek that fronts about 50 or 60 acres of green, green grass. Entrenched Grass Creek curves languidly in its iron-stained bed.

A stone chimney overlooking the rich expanse of meadow is all that is left of a homesteader's cabin. Lots of elk droppings in the vicinity attest to the fact that this trail runs right through the Mount Evans Elk Management Area. Saunter along until you find a likely seat and pause to enjoy meadow ambiance and the snow-furrowed brows of high summits such as Mount Evans and Rogers Peak to the west.

Bear Creek's beauty alone is enough to recommend this trail. But accessing it via Upper Bear Creek Road, which curves past lovely homes, makes the outing even more special. Both the access route and the Grass Creek hike add up to a fine way to get away not far away.

Bluebird/Ponderosa/ Brother Loop

Trail Rating	easy to moderate
Trail Length	2.7-mile loop
Elevation	7,400 to 7,800 feet
Amenities	restrooms
Highlights	June wild iris, fourteener view at high point
Location	Alderfer/Three Sisters Park, Jefferson County Open Space
Directions	From Denver, take I-70 west to CO 74 (Exit 252), and head south. Turn right onto CR 73, take a right on Buffalo Park Road, and proceed 1.5 miles to the parking lot on the right.

Several trails meander through the meadows, conifer forest, and aspen groves of Alderfer/Three Sisters Park, just west of Evergreen. Rock outcroppings and wildflowers accent the landscape along the Bluebird Meadow and Ponderosa Trails leading to "The Brother"—this hike's goal. Views in every direction emanate from the top of The Brother, including a fine one of 14,265-foot Mount Evans.

The large parking area on the park's west boundary is the takeoff point for this hike. Thunderstorms are pretty common occurrences on summer afternoons, so be alert.

Aged ranch buildings attest to this open space's former life, as Bluebird Meadow Trail begins heading east. In June, the wetlands you cross here can be a soothing visual treat of wild iris—our only native Rocky Mountain iris species. Brassy-gold meadow arnica succeeds the iris blooms. Bluebird Trail runs into Silver Fox/Ponderosa Trail where the route turns right. Rugged rock outcrops of silver plume quartz mingle with stout pines, Douglas firs, and slender aspens.

Ponderosa Trail wanders beneath its namesake pines while wildflowers enliven the easygoing walk. As the track undulates along a southern exposure, scrub oak and mountain mahogany cozy up to imposing sun-struck boulders.

Climb left up a short leg of the Sisters Trail to rejoin Ponderosa Trail. Head up left for about 0.3 mile to the spur trail for The Brother to earn distant views. The spur climbs to the worn rock of The Brother's broad summit, where views of his Three Sisters appear to the north. Head to the west side of the humped stone summit for a nice view of fourteener

Mount Evans—particularly attractive when snow-capped. Meadow valleys enhance the foreground. The heady panorama calls for a quiet moment of contemplation or a well-earned snack. Find your own slice of summit bedrock and take a stony seat.

Return down the rocky spur and veer to the right, by some small aspens. Return to the main trail at a junction where the route continues to the right. Along the next part of the trail, where conifers quickly succeed the aspens, ground-hugging kinnikinnick forms vast evergreen mats. In the dry shade of conifers, the trail soon meets more open ponderosa pine parkland. When you return to the wet meadow, take a right onto Bluebird Meadow Trail. Circling the wetland may result in wet feet—worth it for an intimate look at resident wildflowers.

Alderfer/Three Sisters Open Space offers a fine montane experience in the foothills life zone. And when the iris bloom on Bluebird Trail, it's a spirlt-lifting sight.

Evergreen Mountain Loop

Just west of Evergreen, Alderfer/Three Sisters Park, once an old ranch with fine hay meadows, is another jewel in the impressive collection of Jefferson County Open Space. The treasures offered by the hike up Evergreen Mountain include great peak views, excellent exercise, and, in June, purple-blue riches of wild iris at the trail's onset.

The parking area on the north side of Buffalo Park Road is fairly large but can be busy on fine weekends. Plan an early hike for ease of parking and to beat those notorious summer afternoon thunderstorms.

Cross Buffalo Park Road and approach a sloping hay meadow that is seasonally sprinkled with wild iris. These delicate flowers account for the name of the trail, Wild Iris Loop, on which you take a left turn. As you cruise along on crusher-fines, varied wildflowers delight your eyes.

Turn left at the junction with Ranch View Trail. The path curves, traveling past stunted aspens and an outcropping. It subsequently zigzags on a decline. Big ponderosa pines shade a road crossing before the trail wanders by young aspens. Prepare to meet Evergreen Mountain East Trail, where the route turns right.

Under open skies, the trail curves into a drainage and finds another aspen copse

Trail Rating	moderate
Trail Length	5.8-mile loop
Elevation	7,400 to 8,536 feet
Amenities	restrooms
Highlights	views
Location	Alderfer/Three Sisters Park, Jefferson County Open Space
Directions	From Denver, take I-70 west to CO 74 (Exit 252), and head south. Turn right onto CR 73, take another right on Buffalo Park Road, and proceed 1.5 miles to the parking lot on the right.

and its attendant wildflowers, such as scarlet paintbrush. A wide field keeps the wildflower parade marching along with shrubby cinquefoil at the lead.

The trail ascends gently through mixed evergreens onto a north face, granting glimpses of the Evergreen area to the east. Undulating now along an eastern exposure, the track begins switchbacking. Leveling tread precedes lodgepole stands, where a rockier path is flanked by earth-hugging evergreen kinnikinnick mats.

Small ravines appear, offering cool respite from the drier aspects. Where ponderosas dominate, watch for the black, tuft-eared Abert squirrel. Douglas firs then take over as the trail returns to a north face. Not to be outdone, stands of lodgepole enter the conifer fray. The trail coils up to a rugged rock viewpoint and begins a long traverse that leads to the next trail junction.

At this juncture, angle left for a long steady incline on Summit Trail. Views to the south lead to a big broken blister of granite where the track switchbacks rockily on its way to circle Evergreen Mountain's 8,536-foot summit. Begin to the left and loop clockwise on reasonably level trail that leads to a granite outcrop and far views to the west. The rocky top of the mountain allows vistas of the Continental Divide, 14,265-foot Mount Evans and its massif compadres, and closer-in Chief Mountain's 11,709-foot crest.

When you've soaked up those inspiring peak views, continue the circuit of Evergreen Mountain to arrive back at the Summit Loop's start. Retrace your steps to complete the loop until you arrive at a junction, and turn left on Evergreen Mountain West Trail.

Heading on a northwest descent, the trail eases down, via a number of switchbacks, to arrive at the high end of Wild Iris Loop. Take a left here and continue back to the road crossing and your vehicle.

With a fine set of offerings—from vistas to wildflowers, hay meadows to forest—Evergreen Mountain Loop is a fulfilling adventure.

Maxwell Falls

Tucked into a lush drainage west of Evergreen, charming Maxwell Falls is a welcome surprise. Gently pouring the contents of Maxwell Creek over its lip, the small falls culminates a nice little hike in the montane life zone. The only trick to the simple hike is getting to the base of the falling water. This requires a brief stint of rock scrambling—only to find that there's no room at the falls to do more other than admire water sliding down slippery rock. Nonetheless, it's a fun trail to a water feature not commonly found at this low elevation. Boots are advised, especially for the scramble to the base of the falls.

The trail's proximity to Denver makes it a popular destination, so a weekday hike might offer a bit more solitude. The parking pullout accommodates about a dozen vehicles—an early arrival is a good idea. Arriving early also helps beat those oft-occurring summer afternoon thunderstorms.

Heading down from the roadside parking area, the casual trail is flanked by thick meadow grasses. At a sign posting regulations for Arapaho National Forest usage, the path broadens into a road-wide track. Conifers such as Colorado blue spruce and white-barked quaking aspens shade the way as the path drifts down within sound of little Maxwell Creek.

As the track gently descends, riparian vegetation such as willows, and seasonal wildflowers such as black-eyed Susans, are much in evidence. The welcoming creek shows itself where a sign sends the Maxwell Falls Trail straight ahead, while the left fork heads up for Cliff Loop. Meandering amidst towering spruces, Maxwell Creek continues its downward journey while the trail aims uphill briefly before leveling.

Trail Rating	easy, except base of falls
Trail Length	1.2-mile out-and-back
Elevation	8,400 to 8,150 feet
Amenities	none
Highlights	a small close-in waterfall in a sylvan setting
Location	Arapaho National Forest
Directions	From Denver, take I-70 west to CO 74 (Exit 252), and head south. Turn right onto CR 73, proceed 1 mile, and make another right onto South Brook Forest Road (which changes to South Black Mountain Drive). Go 6.4 miles and look for a pullout on the left at the Maxwell Falls Trailhead.

To make its way back to waterway level, the trail S-curves downward, passing jumbled outcrops to reveal a limited canyon-rim view. Make your way down to a worn area between granite boulders and conifers at the top of Maxwell Falls. Although a sign marks Maxwell Falls, the falling water can be more easily heard than seen from here. Bushes and worn outcrops obscure the water, and the effort to view the little falls is hampered by slippery rock and brush. To see Maxwell Falls up close, return to the trail and continue down via switchbacks.

Descending through a stand of lodgepole pine, look on the right toward the creek for a trammeled area between the trees. Search here for the creekside spur path that follows the north bank upstream. Follow the pathway through forest and over boulders until it disappears quite near the falls' base. From here, it is bit of a rock scramble—watch for algae- and moss-slick stones—to attain Maxwell Falls' base. Having arrived, there is limited room to do anything but stand and stare. Across the creek, a great granite overhang acts as guardian.

Maxwell Falls offers a short and sweet jaunt along a finger of Arapaho National Forest poking into Evergreen's outlying residential area. Close to Denver, yet feeling very woodsy, this short trail makes a perfect spur-of-the-moment getaway.

US 285 South

Colorful wildflowers decorate the meadow at Meyer Ranch Open Space.

Coiling southwest through the Front Range, US 285 provides entry into a corridor of evergreen-covered hills and rocky canyons. It also accesses the southern reaches of the Mount Evans Wilderness. Numerous side roads along the way emanate from this fast, convenient passage into the foothills, leading to a handful of seemingly secret hikes.

Several special open space parks lie within this region, including Meyer Ranch, Flying J Ranch, Reynolds, and Pine Valley Ranch. As former homesteads, these plots of land were preserved from development. This good fortune continued when they were acquired by Jefferson County and designated as open space, ensuring their future as pockets of nature for all to enjoy. Today, scenic trails winding through the foothills and montane life zones are available to outdoor enthusiasts and provide great escapes in Denver's diverse backyard.

Contents

US 285 South
Hikes 75 – 81

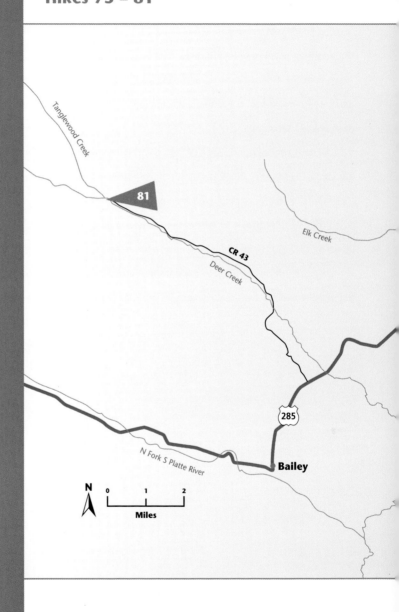

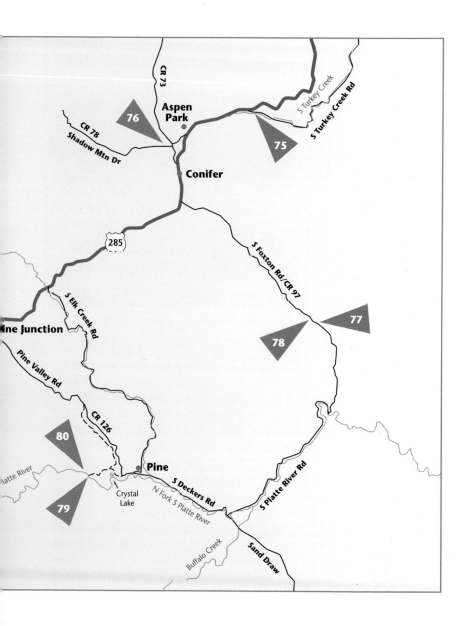

Owl Perch/Lodgepole Loop

Situated in a beautiful valley, Meyer Ranch Park was once a working ranch and part-time ski hill. The lush front meadow teems with wildflowers, and pines shelter the park's higher reaches. The elegant Victorian home across US 285 from the open space is the Meyers' private residence.

Convenient to picnic tables scattered beneath the trees, Owl Perch Trail and Lodgepole Trail form a gentle 2-mile loop that begins and ends by the restrooms. The parking area fills quickly on summer weekends. Arrive early for a spot and to get your hike in before thunderstorms build up on summer afternoons.

For the wildflower aficionado and other lovers of beauty, excitement begins with the first step on the string portion of Owl Perch/Lodgepole Loop. South Turkey Creek flows through a plush meadow where the broad trail is elevated. The wide track turns a corner, then rises gradually through a floristic selection of natives such as dusky purple sugarbowls, waving white bistort, and Colorado blue columbine.

By the time you reach the restroom facilities, the trail has gained about 75 feet in elevation. The trail divides here, and this route heads to the right. At a second junction, the loop heads right again to reach a split log bench shaded by aspens. The pathway meanders up under good-sized ponderosa pines—the favored habitat of tuft-eared Abert squirrels, which are often charcoal black here.

Pines give way to aspens, and a turn to the right at the next junction takes you onto Lodgepole Loop where the sign simply states: trail. A very civilized covered bench looks out over a scene that might inveigle the hiker into a moment's contemplation. The level path now enters mixed conifers. Next, a small drainage dappled by aspen shade leads to a slight rise, lifting the track to another level section

A service road crosses the trail. Stay to the right and continue on Lodgepole Loop. A bit farther, a switchback draws the route up to an area studded with old stumps.

About halfway into the hike, at a junction near the high point, continue straight ahead on Lodgepole Loop as Sunny Aspen Trail climbs off to the right. The track levels along here and leads down toward a drainage. Out in the sun now, the path curves into a little meadow proud of its perfumed wild roses.

Soon after, a trail sign points the loop straight ahead to a sturdy split-log bench in the midst of scarred aspens. The bark of these trees has been scraped by elk, and their teeth marks blacken as fungi get to work. Mosey along to catch a quick view on the left of rugged rock piled up to make a mountain.

Lodgepole Loop heads left at the next trail intersection and descends, via easygoing switchbacks, to sunnier spaces. Rejoin Owl Perch Trail for a gentle descent to the east side of the picnic area. Retracing the balloon loop's string takes you through the flowery entrance meadow again and back to the parking area.

Meyer Ranch Park is close to the metro area in distance, but far away in feeling. Though it is in the foothills life zone, this unique park provides a montane experience.

Trail Rating	easy
Trail Length	2-mile loop
Elevation	7,875 to 8,975 feet
Amenities	restrooms, picnic sites
Highlights	wildflowers, varied habitats
Location	Meyer Ranch, Jefferson County Open Space
Directions	From the junction of C-470 and US 285, southwest of Denver, take US 285 South almost to Aspen Park. Look for a right exit that bends underneath US 285 and onto South Turkey Creek Road. The parking area is immediately on your right.

Junction House/Shadow Pine Loop

Trail Rating	easy
Trail Length	4-mile balloon loop
Elevation	7,900 to 8,200 feet
Amenities	restroom
Highlights	columbine and aspens in June
Location	Flying J Ranch, Jefferson County Open Space/ Denver Mountain Parks
Directions	From the junction of C-470 and US 285, southwest of Denver, take US 285 South to Conifer. Turn right onto CR 73, go just over a mile, and make a left turn onto Shadow Mountain Drive. The trailhead and parking are immediately on the right.

Flying J Ranch sits between Conifer and Evergreen in rolling ponderosa parkland and meadows. Junction House and Shadow Pine Trails combine for an easygoing winding loop behind a montane ranch of dreams—the Flying J. With only 300 feet of elevation gain, this pleasant trail is suitable for most abilities.

Shared with mountain bikers, the small size of the parking area on Shadow Mountain Drive dictates an early arrival, as does the possibility of afternoon thunderstorm activity on summer days.

Begin at the Junction House Trailhead sign off the west end of the parking lot. A map of Flying J Ranch Open Space traces the route your hike will take. Level at first, passing wild roses and bushy potentilla with meadowland on the right, the north-running path winds up onto ponderosa parkland. The black scars on the quaking aspen you'll pass are evidence of foraging elk.

The trail drifts down into the cool shade of conifers before arriving at a sunny wetland expanse. Cross on a well-crafted boardwalk that supports two built-in observation benches. Curve up onto a grassy slope to reach a view of the back side of the Flying J Ranch buildings, including a classic red barn.

The junction of Shadow Pine Loop indicates that you have walked the 0.6-mile "string" part of the route; next comes the 2.8-mile balloon. The route heads right and winds through small lodgepole pines. An aspen grove is accented by a spread of Colorado blue columbine in June, complementing its quaking green canopy.

At the crossing of an old road, follow the Shadow Pine Loop sign on the far side to another view of the picturesque red barn. Enter a mixed conifer forest where a couple of pieces of old farm equipment rest their antique wood and iron bones. A rounded granite outcrop precedes a slight incline that leads to a shaded seasonal creek. In June, you might find the delicate pink arrows of shooting stars here.

The trail forks in a gentle meadow where this route heads left. Closely ranked or "dog hair" lodgepole pine surround a cruising segment. Ease down to a small ravine where outcrops boast legions of lichen. The 8,200-foot high point is not far from a switchback that turns the loop to a south heading. The trail undulates through varying landscape—from forest and lush aspen glades to dry rocky stretches and sparsely vegetated slopes—before entering a section where wildflowers thrive in the dappled shade of deep grasses and tall aspen.

A recently burned area reveals that the natural recovery process is jump-started by quick-response wildflowers such as golden smoke, strawberry blite, and scorpionweed. After crossing the ranch road, the trail drifts down to rejoin the Junction House portion of the route.

Close-in and tranquil on an easygoing gradient, the trails in Flying J Open Space offer the hiker a sneak peek at foothill and montane ranchland.

Hummingbird/Songbird Loop

Reynolds Park is another jewel in the Jefferson County Open Space crown. The park spans a wide variety of habitats including lush riparian, grassy meadows, warm, dry south-facing slopes, and protected north faces of fir and spruce. The loop formed by Hummingbird and Songbird Trails lies within the foothills life zone. Much of it crosses a south exposure, making it a good early season hike. One of the loop's rewards is an unexpected view of Pikes Peak framed in a canyon gap.

Shared by picnickers' vehicles, the parking area is adequate. Keep a weather eye peeled for thunderstorms, which often occur on summer afternoons and can sneak up on you.

From the parking area, head east across CR 97 where Hummingbird Trail takes off to the right up an abandoned road. It is a steady climb until the trail forks right, leaving the old roadway. The southwest exposure here harbors shrubs such as mountain mahogany and wax currant, which flourish in the xeric habitat. Aromatic junipers also populate the slope. The berries —actually cones—of female junipers flavor game and gin.

Though not common on hot south-facing exposures, a few Douglas firs stand sentinel along the steep rocky slope where drought-resistant wildflowers bloom. The track becomes fairly level as it aims toward a sharp

Trail Rating	moderate
Trail Length	1.9-mile loop
Elevation	7,200 to 7,400 feet
Amenities	picnic tables, restrooms
Highlights	Pikes Peak peek, varied habitats
Location	Reynolds Park, Jefferson County Open Space
Directions	From the junction of US 285 and C-470 in southwest Denver, head south on US 285 for about 13 miles through Conifer. Turn left on South Foxton Road (CR 97). Reynolds Park is 5.1 miles down the road, and parking is on the right.

corner revealing a short, stone-paved shelf on the right. Ball cactus adds character to the bedrock peninsula. From here you can view the trails on Reynolds Park's west side.

As the route crosses a scrub oak saddle, look straight ahead to see a uniquely framed view of Pikes Peak. The massive fourteener is particularly stunning from this angle, especially when it's snow-capped. According to the latest elevation calculations, it now rises 14,115 feet.

Gentle switchbacks descend along the north side of the saddle into the welcome shade of big Douglas firs and scrub oak. A seasonal creek may be heard in spring. This is a lovely and secluded spot for a snack or a snooze.

Moving out into the open again, descend a dry slope dotted with silvery, aromatic fringed sage. The red buildings to the south were part of an old dude ranch and are now used by the park. Once across the county road, begin the Songbird portion of the loop by heading right. Pass a few picnic tables on the way to a wooden bridge spanning a creek. Saunter the shady stretch back to the parking area on a pleasant riparian trail.

With the soothing hues of winsome violets and refined blue columbine, the level shady path feels cool as it parallels Kennedy Gulch Creek. The loop finishes along the northern exposure of serene Songbird Trail. Back at the picnic area, hikers can slake their thirst at an old-fashioned pump or choose a streamside picnic table for a well-earned repast.

Reynolds Park manages to pack a lot of floral and scenic variety into just a few miles of trail. A visit, particularly when Hummingbird/Songbird Loop is dressed in spring finery, is a fulfilling outing.

Oxen Draw/Eagle's View/ Raven's Roost Loop

Trail Rating	moderate
Trail Length	3.4-mile loop
Elevation	7,200 to 8,100 feet
Amenities	restrooms, picnic sites, water pump
Highlights	diversity, wildflowers, Pikes Peak view
Location	Reynolds Park, Jefferson County Open Space
Directions	From the junction of US 285 and C-470 in southwest Denver, head south on US 285 for about 13 miles through Conifer. Turn left on South Foxton Road (CR 97). Reynolds Park is 5.1 miles down the road, and parking is on the right.

Reynolds Park's transition zone gives hikers a taste of overlapping foothills life zone and montane elevations. Contained in the park's 1,200-plus acres are riparian habitats, deep forest shade, rocky outcrops, xeric spaces, and ridge-top grasslands. The hike is highlighted by the Eagle's View spur trail— well worth the extra effort for the panorama of Pikes Peak.

Reynolds Park maps are available at the east edge of the parking area by Kennedy Gulch Creek. Note the Oxen Draw shortcut, which begins at a trail sign near the restrooms. Parking is generous. Summer afternoon thunderstorms are a possibility, so keep an eye on the sky.

Oxen Draw Trail, accompanied by a small creek, soon makes the first of a dozen water crossings. Take the first left after crossing the creek, and before long a second crossing is reached. A meadow area on the right supports an attractive but aggressive Eurasian import—butter 'n eggs or common toadflax.

At a junction marked by signpost, take a right. Soon the loop heads left following Oxen Draw Trail, which now labors uphill under the cool shade of Colorado blue spruce and Douglas fir. Long-spurred blue columbine enjoys the filtered shade of the forest floor. Look for shooting stars' pink arrows near the next two creek crossings.

Before starting up by a steep rockfall area on the right, listen for the cooling sound of cascading water among big blocks of stone. Rougher and rockier now, the path reaches a small causeway. Alder, Rocky Mountain maple, and blue spruce line the rocky waterway on the way to yet another crossing of the stream. In June, look for spurless blue columbine, a variation of the famous Colorado state flower.

After a couple more of those stride-wide creek crossings, Oxen Draw Trail leads up to the Eagle's View spur trail. Rising to a panoramic view of Pikes Peak, this shady side trail is worth every step. On top, the bird's-eye view is of 14,115-foot Pikes Peak far to the south.

Back at the spur's junction, the loop heads east on Raven's Roost Trail. Cross over the creek one more time to reach a fairly easy trail segment that traverses a warm south-facing slope. Raven's Roost runs into an old roadway and the trail swings left as it drops steadily before joining Elkhorn Trail. A bench placed in a small saddle makes a nice rest stop.

On the way down, the trail levels briefly before switchbacks descend to the next stage. The switchback section is short, and the route becomes easygoing as it nears the banks of Kennedy Gulch Creek. Restrooms lie just ahead. Beyond them is a picnic area and a pump that gushes refreshingly cool water.

Reynolds Park is an hour—and worlds away—from the Denver-metro area. Its Oxen Draw/Eagle's View/Raven's Roost Loop offers a fine diversity of hiking and wildflowering experience.

Park View

Tucked into a beautiful secluded valley with the crystalline North Fork of the South Platte River running through it, Pine Valley Ranch is a find. Once a private enclave, the approximately 800 acres now invite picnickers, anglers, stargazers, and hikers. Park View Trail is designated for hikers and climbs 430 feet in under a mile, making it fairly aerobic. A wayside overlook shows off the property's lodge, designed in the style of Germany's Black Forest manors. The observatory, which tops a knoll like a dark toadstool, offers star programs. Registration for these programs is at Jefferson County's Lookout Mountain headquarters in Golden.

Parking in paved lots on several levels is generous. Since this lovely site has fairly limited horizon views, it is best to be alert for changes in weather. Watch for signs of the notorious thunderstorms that build up on summer afternoons. Dogs are not permitted on Park View Trail.

Orient yourself at the trail sign at the west end of the lowest parking lot, or pick up a map here to take with you. An artfully rusted bridge spans the alluring North Fork, beckoning the hiker to cross. Turn left along the riverside concrete path to Pine Lake.

At the south corner of the little fishing lake a set of timber steps starts off Park View Trail. The track then turns west on natural surface tread and climbs steadily. Along the way, wild raspberries tempt hikers in late July and offer food for wildlife. Colonizing wild raspberry is one of the first plants to heal burned areas, and they currently thrive in this area, recently swept by

Trail Rating	moderate
Trail Length	1.6-mile out-and-back
Elevation	6,820 to 7,250 feet
Amenities	restrooms, fishing decks, picnic sites
Highlights	secluded valley, clear river, hiker-only trail, naturalist-led activities
Location	Pine Valley Ranch, Jefferson County Open Space
Directions	From the junction of US 285 and C-470 in southwest Denver, head south on US 285 for about 20 miles to Pine Junction. Turn left on Pine Valley Road (CR 126), and proceed 5.8 miles to Crystal Lake Road—a hairpin turn on the right just after a sign for Pine Valley Ranch.

fire. As you trek through blackened spots, note the stark contrast between Pine Valley Park's natural lushness and the vast mountainside stretches of standing snags.

Timber steps elevate the path to outcrop clusters, revealing the river-grateful green heart of the park below. From the railed overlook, the 1927 lodge, built in the style of Germany's Black Forest manors, can be viewed.

A series of stairs reveals more raspberry colonies on the way up to an imposing rock outcrop shouldering the trail into tight submission. The curved railing and well-crafted stairway are helpful at this precarious point. Sweeping bird's-eye views of the burned and the unburned continue to remind us of the fragility of life. The serene river flows below.

Pine Valley Park Open Space is a cherished place that we appreciate even more because much of it was spared the ravages of fire. The Park View Trail brings out a particular awareness of our good fortune.

Pine Lake/North Fork View/ Narrow Gauge

From the towering spires of Colorado blue spruce and the clear North Fork of the South Platte River to the varied hiking trails, nice picnic facilities, and small fishable lake, Pine Valley Ranch has much to entice visitors. This 800-plus-acre Jefferson County Open Space Park, cupped in a river-carved canyon, offers over 5 miles of trail including the multi-use Narrow Gauge Trail and the hiker-only North Fork View and Pine Lake Trails. The figure eight formed by these trails is nearly level, making it great for young children and folks who like to saunter.

Varying naturalist-led activities also occur here, including star shows in the old observatory on the property. Call Jeffco Open Space's Lookout Mountain Nature Center headquarters in Golden for more information on these programs. A gazebo and several picnic shelters—one with 15 tables—are available for reservation.

Paved parking is on three levels. (The topmost is set up for horse trailers.) Watch for building thunderstorms on summer afternoons.

A sylvan scene presents itself as the North Fork of the South Platte River, lined by courtly blue spruces, flows tranquilly below. To begin the double loop, walk to the west end of the lower parking lot and cross the river on an arced bridge. Turn left onto a wide concrete pathway, enjoying the shining river shaded by big Colorado blue spruces. Curving around to the west brings you by a stone shelter. Stay straight ahead along the south shore of Pine Lake.

The little lake is regularly stocked with fish and offers grassy banks for angling and relaxing. Wildflowers spangle the trail-sides as you reach a bench overlooking Pine Lake. A trio of fishing decks lays the foreground for

Trail Rating	easy
Trail Length	1.5-mile figure eight
Elevation	6,850 feet
Amenities	restrooms, picnic sites, naturalist-led activities
Highlights	clear river, fishing pond
Location	Pine Valley Ranch, Jefferson County Open Space
Directions	From the junction of US 285 and C-470 in southwest Denver, head south on US 285 for about 20 miles to Pine Junction. Turn left on Pine Valley Road (CR 126), and proceed 5.8 miles to Crystal Lake Road—a hairpin turn on the right just after a sign for Pine Valley Ranch.

the dramatic home perched on the hillside. This home, now known as the Pine Valley Ranch Lodge, was built in the style of Germany's Black Forest manors. Behind the bench, a slope exhibits the ravages of wildfire.

The west end of the lake hosts an emerald wetland zone. The roadway turns, bringing you to a junction where a sign directs hikers to the left. Soon an old-fashioned water pump marks the spot where the North Fork View Trail can be accessed. Cross an alluvial fan of decomposed golden granite— probably the result of flash flood activity ripping through fire-stripped earth. The trail is less defined here as it curves to the west through a scenic meadow full of tall grasses. The track, wending between hillside and riverside, enters a timeless scene.

Wade through the verdant meadow on a barely visible trail. Meadowbound spruces mark a section of crusher fines sandwiched between timbers. As you approach a bridge, a line of stately spruces enters the picture.

Travel over the peridot-green North Fork to meet the Narrow Gauge portion of the hike. This trail follows the 1878 railroad grade of the Denver, Leadville and Gunnison Railroad, installed to haul ice in the first decade of the 1900s.

Pass through wildflowers, wild hops, and willows before another bridge and a sign turn the loop right, back to Pine Lake. As you pass between the river and the lake, look to the right to spot an old beaver lodge. Continue along the lakeshore to the east end, descend stairs to river-level, and return to the hike's beginning.

A gem that reflects the shining forethought of Jefferson County's Open Space Parks plan, Pine Valley Ranch, with its bright lake and river, is worthy of placement in a crown.

Tanglewood

Trail Rating	moderate
Trail Length	4.4-mile out-and-back
Elevation	9,250 to 10,440 feet
Amenities	none
Highlights	tumbling creek, wildflowers
Location	Mount Evans Wilderness, Pike National Forest
Directions	From the junction of US 285 and C-470 in southwest Denver, head south on US 285 for about 25 miles. Look for a right turn onto CR 43 about 5 miles past Pine Junction. Proceed for 6.8 miles, bear left at the fork, and continue to Deer Creek Campground. Bear right at the creek crossing and continue to the trailhead at the end of the road.

Lively Tanglewood Creek accompanies this gentle-becoming-aerobic trail into Mount Evans Wilderness and Pike National Forest. The Deer Creek Trailhead, about an hour into the mountains southwest of the Denver-metro area, is host to the Tanglewood Trail. This route enters a tight stream valley, where the landscape alternates between forest and flowery pocket meadows. From late June into July, Tanglewood could be called "shooting star trail," for the lovely pink blooms that thrive along this route. Boots help mitigate the impact of wet or rocky trail stretches.

The parking area is shared with horse trailers and fills quickly on weekends. Plan to arrive early. Those infamous thunder-and-lightning storms can brew up quickly on summer afternoons.

Lush pasture grasses surround the parking area where Tanglewood Trail breaches a gap in the fence. A sign announces access to Mount Evans Wilderness.

The stony old roadbed travels among aspen and wildflowers. Soon a sign inscribed Tanglewood Trail #636 sends hikers on a level stretch into the shade of Colorado blue spruce. As you prepare to cross a split-log bridge spanning sparkling Tanglewood Creek, a mossy embankment on the left displays a few June-blooming calypso orchids.

Ferns flourish on a lichen-encrusted outcrop, and hot-pink shooting stars are particularly prevalent through this section. Flat now, the track paces along the east side of the creek.

Return to the west side via a plank bridge that deposits hikers at a sweet pink and white garden. Continue up to a culvert funneling water under the trail. Quaking aspens lead toward timeless bristlecone pines. These remarkable pines may live thousands of years. Their bottlebrush needle arrangement is characteristically flecked with pungent resin—a protective "dandruff" that puts off foragers such as mule deer.

A narrowing tread penetrates a mixed forest, where a damp environment supports shooting stars. Spanning the creek, a split log sends the hiker alongside stair-stepping waters. The stony trail heads up to an old iron pipe beside another garden of. . .yes. . .shooting stars.

Alternating stretches of forest and meadow lead the hiker up to a sign, at approximately the 1-mile mark, incised with the words Mount Evans Wilderness. At a junction, a second sign indicates that Tanglewood Trail continues straight ahead. Advancing adjacent to the creek, hikers face a huff-and-puff pitch assisted by peeled log risers. Before pulling up on a rocky tread, an easygoing streamside segment offers more flowery arenas. Travel back into mixed forest where a log bridges a side stream

Matched logs placed side by side form the "corduroy" road that once carried wagon wheels over boggy stretches. Note the wild strawberries filling the open spots near one of these decaying sections of road.

Rocky, rugged, and rising now, the track acquits itself among fore-shortened spruces. Hidden by willows, Tanglewood Creek verifies its presence with soothing sound. Soon a big log spans the waterway, offering a momentary respite from uphilling.

An inviting meadow, reportedly the site of an old sawmill, invites hikers to relax and contemplate the contentment of a mission accomplished. This creek-side meadow is the turnaround point for this description. (The trail ascends more seriously from here on, eventually arriving at Roosevelt Lakes in another 2.5 miles.)

Wildflowers, water, and the wisdom gained from walking in the wild make Tanglewood Trail a quality hike. The rushing creek heightens awareness and instills a sense of freedom and accomplishment.

Chatfield/Roxborough Area

The Fountain Formation complements
a spring display of golden banner in
Roxborough State Park.

Nestled against a flank of Pike National Forest to the west, and nearly surrounded by suburbia, this region on the southwest edge of Denver provides close-in getaways that make for ready escapes when time is of the essence. The diverse environments here range from red-rock to riverine, with forests and meadows in between.

Chatfield State Park's distinctive nature trails wind through the South Platte's riparian habitats, while scenic Waterton Canyon marks the spot where the river surges down from the Rockies on its way to the Great Plains. Roxborough State Park's sandstone spires of the Lyons and Fountain Formations highlight the area a bit farther south, providing a gorgeous glimpse into geologic history. South Valley and Deer Creek Canyon Open Space Parks offer numerous peaceful trails to the southwest, featuring sandstone formations of their own. This region is a truly special place for the hurried, harried, and hassled to recharge their batteries by hiking through Denver's hinterland.

Contents

Chatfield/Roxborough Area

Hikes 82 – 94

S Deer Creek Canyon Rd

S Platte River Rd

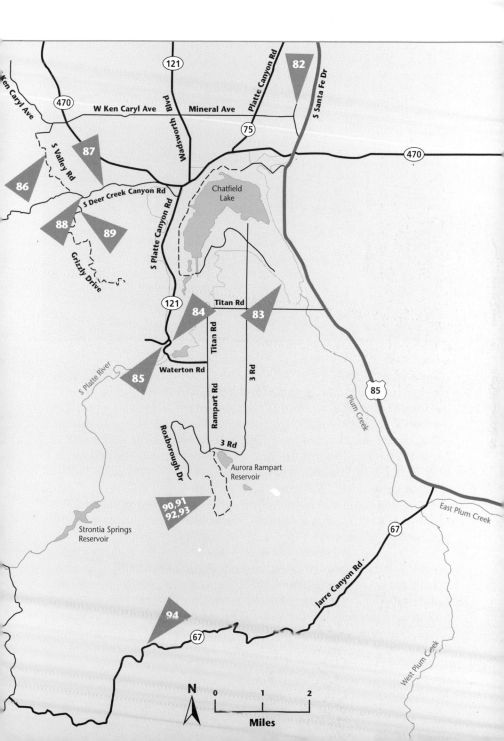

Northern Wildlife Loop

Once a fine log home, the Carson Nature Center is a wonderful place to explore before you set out on the Northern Wildlife Loop. A wide variety of nature programs are offered by the kid-friendly facility, and, in addition to inanimate displays, there are tanks of native fish, snakes, and turtles. The convenient hike itself provides a close-up look at the waterfowl and wading birds that frequent the South Platte River; bring binoculars for an even better view. This park is easily reached via RTD Light Rail's Mineral Avenue station.

Parking becomes very competitive on weekends. Plan an early hike in order to secure a space and avoid the crowds, and watch for thunderstorms on summer afternoons.

Begin your riverside walk by heading west from the parking area's map kiosk, via a short stretch of concrete pathway. A narrow connector trail crosses the Platte Greenway's concrete sidewalk to reach the embankment standing above the South Platte River. A post is signed: River Access. Turn right, along the somewhat obscure footpath once defined by chipped bark. This is the string of the balloon loop.

Willow bushes lead the way along the water where mallards and other ducks dabble. Keep a lookout for the great blue heron and its smaller cousin, the black-crowned night-heron.

Enter a segment of hiker-only trail on the other side of a split-rail fence. Drift down to reach a fork, and begin the balloon portion of the nature loop by heading left toward the river. An arrow on a post confirms the way.

Pass above the river on an embankment, and look below for Canada geese and ducks that like to congregate on sand spits. Exposed snags rise above a big tree on the far bank—a favorite spot of cormorants. This is a good place to stop and see what avian species your binoculars find.

Wend your way through junglelike vegetation such as wild hop vine. The continuing trail gladdens you with birdsong and sightings. The river bends in a curve and the path crosses a sturdy timber span over a bit of clear water.

Big cottonwood patriarchs mark the place where the loop takes a strong right and heads for a little footbridge. Another right turn keeps you on the loop, heading south. Cottontail rabbits dash about in the cool shade of overarching trees and disappear in the grasses and shrubbery. Golden currant, honeysuckle, and chokecherry fruits supply food for wildlife here.

An open space reveals civilization before you head back beneath the leafy canopy. Watch for a nice view of the Front Range in the distant west. You'll soon rejoin to the string of the balloon, where you can retrace your steps to the parking lot.

Gentle and peaceful, this short loop offers a suburban retreat along the South Platte River. If you didn't take advantage of the Carson Nature Center before you started the Northern Wildlife Loop, give it a go when you return.

Trail Rating	easy
Trail Length	1.4-mile balloon loop
Elevation	5,360 feet
Amenities	restrooms
Highlights	Carson Nature Center, South Platte River, birds
Location	South Platte Park
Directions	From C-470 southwest of Denver, exit at Santa Fe Drive (US 85) and head north. Turn left on Mineral Avenue, continue for 0.2 mile, and turn right onto South Platte River Parkway. Proceed to road's end at the nature center and parking lot.

Turtle Pond

Chatfield State Park is a popular outdoor venue in the swelling suburbs of southwest Littleton. Boaters, campers, picnickers, strollers, fisherfolk, bird-watchers, beach aficionados, and sunset devotees are drawn to Chatfield Reservoir's waters and adjacent recreation sites. Some areas in the park get quite crowded, but lesser-known spots, such as Turtle Pond, offer solitude.

Watch for deer grazing along the approach road in the early or late hours of the day. The park's South Platte River inlet serves as a line of species demarcation, with white-tailed deer on the east and mule deer on the west. Birdwatchers might glimpse great blue herons cruising gracefully overhead.

Parking in the paved lot at road's end is rarely a problem. The wide-open flats make it fairly easy for hikers to spot thunderstorms building on the horizon.

Look for brown posts flanking the trammeled path off the southwest end of the parking area. The trail leads south from here across the grass-dominated flats. Follow it through meadowland, passing cattail domains as the route turns east and connects with an asphalt pathway. A turn to the right will head you in the direction of Turtle Pond in Chatfield State Park's Plum Creek Nature Area.

Cottonwood patriarchs and willows enjoy their riparian habitat and shade the banks of braided Plum Creek. The trees also provide habitat for various species of birds, drawing enthusiastic birders to the wilder zones of Chatfield State Park. Evidence of beaver busywork abounds along the route.

Trail Rating	easy
Trail Length	1.5-mile out-and-back
Elevation	5,400 feet
Amenities	restrooms (at park entrance)
Highlights	small pond and large marsh area
Location	Chatfield State Park
Directions	From C-470 southwest of Denver, take the Wadsworth Boulevard exit, head south, and turn left into Chatfield State Park. Turn right after the entry station, circle to the marina turnoff, and take the first right to the paved road's end. There is a fee to enter the park.

Wend along the pathway and come to a "Y" intersection in a copse of cottonwoods. The trail to the right may be taken on the return trip for a longer hike—actually a loop—that partially utilizes the spur road upon which you drove to the parking area. However, for the described route, stay to the left and curve around until a straightaway suddenly delivers you to Turtle Pond.

Frogs as big as saucers, turtles as boxy as birthday presents, and dragonflies striped like acrobatic biplanes call this pond home. So does a portly muskrat. A few minutes of quiet observation from the steep-banked levee surrounding the water might reveal other creatures such as an occasional pair of mallard ducks.

The trail ends at the vast cattail marsh mooring the south end of Turtle Pond. This swamp of tall cattails has beavers to thank for its creation. In spring, great flocks of red-winged blackbirds claim the marsh and fill the air with a burbling cacophony of new-season song.

Though not long, the trail to Turtle Pond in Chatfield State Park's hinterland invites you to discover less-visited wildlife habitat. Kids will be especially taken with the critters that live here. Morning or evening, when wildlife is most active, is the best time to enjoy this short and easy hike.

Hike 84

Audubon Discovery Loop

At the south end of Chatfield State Park, a picturesque pair of historic stone buildings, now owned by the Audubon Society, mark the trailhead of the Audubon Discovery Loop. Hikers can visit a series of wetland ponds, often dotted with waterfowl. Bird-watchers should be sure to bring binoculars, as over 300 bird species wing their way among the ponds and riparian woods along this stretch of the South Platte River. This loop is ideal for an early morning saunter when avian species are most active. Some fine sunsets may be enjoyed here, too.

In addition to Muskrat and Blackbird Ponds, the 2.5-mile loop includes a boardwalk and wetlands observation gazebo. The circuit has little elevation change, which makes for an easygoing walk.

Parking is generous in the Lockheed Martin Discovery Pavilion lot. Summer afternoons are ripe for gathering thunderstorms, so keep an eye on the weather if you hike later in the day.

Passing the convenient restrooms east of the parking area, look for the loop's start, marked with brown split rails and a sign for Audubon Discovery Loop Trail and points beyond. Hike east through a bounty of rabbitbrush, which blooms yellow-gold in late summer. Practically hidden by sandbar willow and wild grapevines, Muskrat Pond will be on your left. Box elder trees, members of the maple family, define the right side of the trail. Crusher-fines lead around Muskrat Pond's east end where wild grapevines run rampant over waterside vegetation.

A fork in the trail sends the loop left, and you will see an observation deck across the water. Take the cattail-flanked boardwalk to the far side of Muskrat Pond where the loop turns right. Follow the west shore of Blackbird Pond along a path called Animal Tracks Trail. This rippling pond sports stone-protected coves scooped out for fishing and wildlife observation.

Animal Tracks Trail turns to the east and heads through small cottonwoods and willows via a minor footbridge, returning hikers to the main trail again. A turn to the left brings a long pond into view, and the loop tracks on its east bank. This larger body of water, refered to as Island Pond, is a great place to spot waterfowl.

About the same time the South Platte River delineates the route's right flank, a social trail comes in from the right. Pass this unmarked path, and watch for eroding banks as you make your way through a narrowing neck of land between the river and the pond.

Drifting along close to the river, the trail heads into cottonwoods and uses a raised levee for passage. Follow the singletrack trail, watching for occasional poison ivy. Upon reaching an intersection, turn left and regain a wider route that passes shade trees.

Cross a wide grassy meadow where another left turn, this time onto a narrow crusher-fines surface, curves around to the observation gazebo. This small loop under open skies is flanked with native grasses such as blue grama, affectionately called eyelash grass.

At the gazebo, a sign discusses the terraced wetlands below—a favorite dining area for many species of ducks and other water birds. The side loop joins a roadway where a left turn takes you back to your vehicle.

Easygoing hiking, opportunities to observe wildlife, and the water's siren call make this hike a winner.

Trail Rating	easy
Trail Length	2.5-mile balloon loop
Elevation	5,430 feet
Amenities	restrooms
Highlights	wetlands boardwalk, observation gazebo, waterfowl viewing
Location	Chatfield State Park
Directions	From C-470 southwest of Denver, take the Wadsworth Boulevard exit and head south. Turn left on Waterton Road and left again into the Lockheed Martin Discovery Pavilion parking area.

Hike 85

Waterton Canyon

Waterton Canyon is a special place. Where else in the greater Denver metro area do you have a chance to see bighorn sheep up close? It is also the beginning of the 470-mile-long Colorado Trail which stretches from Denver to Durango. Major Stephen Long's 1820 expedition is said to have made camp here at the mouth of the South Platte. He would be surprised to see how his lonely camping spot now attracts tens of thousands of visitors each year. This heavily used canyon follows a road that eventually arrives at the Strontia Springs Dam, although this hike ends 2 miles before, at the Marston Diversion Dam.

Bikers, hikers, and fisherfolk share the big parking area across the road from the trailhead with equestrians, birders, and picnickers. From the confines of a canyon it is difficult to watch the horizon for afternoon thunderstorms, so they might appear suddenly. Be prepared. Dogs are not permitted in Waterton Canyon.

Leaving the fenced parking area, head west across busy Waterton Road and proceed to the trailhead sign and Waterton Canyon map. Cross a paved zone. The white buildings and dry ponds on the left make up the Kassler Water Plant.

A mass of hoary old cottonwoods shade scattered picnic tables at the mouth of the canyon. Autumn turns these great trees molten gold, especially beautiful when illumined by sunlight. The wide road, following the 1877 narrow-gauge bed of the Denver South Park and Pacific Railroad, takes hikers toward the canyon-confined South Platte River.

Willows take over once your riverside journey begins. Keep an eye out for a plump robin-sized bird—the water ouzel or American dipper. Bobbing on water-bound rocks, it prepares to pop in and stroll along the river bottom, looking for dinner. Kingfishers, chattering in flight, may be heard as they arrow along the river looking for a meal.

Once you've passed under a pipeline, you've entered true bighorn sheep habitat. Scan the rocks above for the well-camouflaged bighorns. Their white rumps make spotting possible.

Carving its canyon ever deeper, the South Platte runs over a rocky bed as it turns a corner at a check dam. Picnic tables and restroom facilities anchor the broad spot. This is a great place for children to explore and appreciate nature's river environment.

Willows guard the waterway as it passes a side canyon and a dip. Canyon walls fall back a bit, broadening the towering scene, as a bend marks the 2.5-mile point. More picnic facilities and another restroom are across the way from a water-management residence.

Following curvaceous canyon contours, the trail brings visitors up to a lacy sheet of water flowing evenly down the slanted concrete face of Marston Diversion Dam. A quiet pool winds back behind the dam face, presenting fine reflections on a still day. This hike reaches the 4-mile mark and its turnaround point here, although the road continues to Strontia Springs Dam.

Rugged canyon walls flanking the sparkling South Platte River make for spectacular scenery on this hike through Waterton Canyon. The outing is especially fulfilling when noble Rocky Mountain bighorns make an appearance.

Trail Rating	easy
Trail Length	8-mile out-and-back
Elevation	5,500 to 5,600 feet
Amenities	restrooms, picnic tables
Highlights	bighorn sheep, steep river canyon
Location	Waterton Canyon
Directions	From C-470 southwest of Denver, take the Wadsworth Boulevard exit and head south. Turn left on Waterton Road and proceed 0.3 mile to the parking area on the left. The trailhead is across the road.

Swallow/Coyote Song/ Lyons Back/Columbine/ Cathy Johnson Loop

Trail Rating	easy to moderate
Trail Length	3.5-mile balloon loop
Elevation	5,950 to 6,070 to 5,850 feet
Amenities	restrooms and picnic shelters are slightly off the route
Highlights	scenic red sandstone Fountain Formation, wildflowers
Location	South Valley Park, Jefferson County Open Space; Ken Caryl Ranch Foundation
Directions	From C-470 southwest of Denver, exit at West Ken Caryl Avenue and head west. Turn left at the light onto South Valley Road and proceed 1.2 miles. Make another left at the sign for South Valley Park.

Just west of Littleton, a southwest suburb of Denver, is a unique bit of Jefferson County Open Space called South Valley Park. It offers a number of trails, including this loop, which shares ground administered by the Ken Caryl Ranch Foundation. Swallow/Coyote Song Trail launches hikers among prows of red Fountain Formation sandstone, extensive scrub oak copses, and open meadows. Both plains and foothills wildflowers thrive here in the transition life zone. A late May or early June outing is suggested for wildflowers. Repeated elevation gains and losses give this hike its "moderate" designation.

Parking, shared by other outdoor enthusiasts, is generous. A weekday hike sees fewer mountain bikers and hikers, and thus offers a more quiet experience. Watch for those infamous thunderstorms on summer afternoons.

Before ascending the stairs that initiate the Swallow connector to Coyote Song Trail, consult the map kiosk and pick up a trail guide. Juts and bubbles of sandstone, rusted red from iron oxide, contrast with emerald Gambel oak, more commonly called scrub oak. Luminous stalks of orchid penstemon complement both rock and oak in early spring. Sparse-tailed rock squirrels might catch your eye as they scamper over rough sandstone hoodoos.

The track leads to a junction that aims Coyote Song Trail to the right before the loop heads left along Lyons Back Trail. Ascending, the route leads along a warm exposure enhanced by raw red soil—the perfect foil for hot-blue larkspur. Dip under scrub oak and rise to a prominent outcrop on the right for a great view of the Ken Caryl Valley and the forested foothills beyond. In the company of junipers, rock stairs lift hikers up to bedrock footing on a south-facing slope where prickly pear cactus makes its home. A small drainage takes the trail up to the Lyons Back Trail saddle, where a sign designates a jurisdiction change from Jefferson County Open Space to land managed by the Ken Caryl Ranch Foundation.

A view of the Dakota Hogback opens to the east, and the loop takes a left, heading down and north along Columbine Trail. Leveling and keeping left, the trail reveals glowing orange paintbrush. The track inclines alongside a rocky spine, then evens out amidst mountain mahogany and scrub oak.

Open skies and a gentle rise precede a winding, oak-flanked decline sequined with spring wildflowers. A long, grass-dominated valley, flanked by the Lyons Formation and the Dakota Hogback, takes you onto the roadlike Cathy Johnson Trail. Head right, paralleling a vertical rock face to the east; its heights may resound with the distinctive descending trill of the canyon wren. Cruise this segment to reach the power line, and watch for your return trail angling back to the right. The trail ascends a ridge and passes through an area of white limestone outcrop before reaching a junction. Head left here, on the Columbine Trail again, to complete the balloon portion of the hike. Ease up to the ridge saddle and return the way you came.

Close enough for an evening hike or early morning jaunt, South Valley Park is a sweet space to enjoy a quick refreshing immersion into nature. A pleasurable walk at this southwest-metro site is enhanced by views, showy rock formations, and flowers.

Coyote Song/Swallow Loop

Red sandstone and arching hogback ridges characterize the scenic setting of South Valley Park. Grasslands and scrub oak complement the massive walls and hoodoos coloring 2.8-mile Coyote Song/Swallow Loop. Elk and deer frequent the area.

Undulating most of the way, the Coyote Song Trail slowly ascends some 300 vertical feet. Then it drops onto hiker-only Swallow Trail, which is level for most of its length. Picnic sites and restrooms are available at the north end of Swallow Trail.

Parking is good in the lot adjacent to South Deer Creek Canyon Road. The possibility of summer afternoon thunderstorms should be considered.

At the trailhead sign, pick up a map to South Valley Park and locate the Coyote Song/Swallow Loop. Start up the string of the balloon loop on a sandy trail.

Ancient rock formations stand like natural gates, bidding you to enter their realm. Grassland featuring several native species such as big bluestem surrounds the track. Patches of Gambel oak, commonly called scrub oak, dot the area.

Cresting, the trail exposes the futuristic silver building that houses Lockheed Martin's Deer Creek Facility. Another rise places you in a meadow vale, surrounded by slabs of iron-oxide-stained Fountain Formation. Cruising along this scenic lesson in 300-million-year-old rock, the trail arrives at a fork where the balloon portion of the loop begins. Bear right on to Coyote Song Trail and continue to enjoy the widening view, replete with seasonal wildflowers.

Trail Rating	easy
Trail Length	2.8-mile balloon loop
Elevation	5,700 to 6,000 feet
Amenities	restrooms
Highlights	red sandstone fins, wildflower-splotched grasslands
Location	South Valley Park, Jefferson County Open Space
Directions	From C-470 southwest of Denver, take the Wadsworth Boulevard exit and head south 0.2 mile to South Deer Creek Canyon Road. Turn right and proceed to the trailhead and parking area on the right.

Climb easily into shrublands fortified by sculptured rock, including the wall of petrified sand dunes known as the Lyons Formation. But the reds of the Fountain Formation truly captivate the eye. Eroded by the elements since they were pushed up from deep in the earth over 65 million years ago, these depositional remnants were once the Ancestral Rockies.

Passing the Lyons Back Trail, continue to the north on Coyote Song and find yourself swooping into another grassy swale. Coming up on another junction, turn left and continue toward hiker-only Swallow Trail. Head downhill in a northwest direction where, off to the right, you'll find picnic shelters and tables with marvelous views. The alternate picnic area and rest-rooms are below.

Take a left where the hiker-only portion of Swallow Trail heads south on crusher-fines. Level and even underfoot, this pleasant cruising trail soon passes tiny Mann Reservoir. A sandstone face towers to the left—white streaks on red rock are evidence of avian occupation. If you look carefully, you can spot the swallows' mud nests built high up on the wall. This trail is aptly named.

A grove of cottonwoods and a few willows appears on the right, then the trail passes through a disturbed area full of wooly mullein, a favorite food source of hairy and downy woodpeckers as well as chickadees. A left at the next intersection leads back to the string where you can retrace your steps to your vehicle.

For a fast hike or a leisurely stroll among striking rock formations, try the Coyote Song/Swallow Loop.

Grazing Elk Loop

South Valley Park is an area of archeological and geological merit with several scenic trails. Grazing Elk Trail is situated on a grassland bench in the west section of the park and cruises through elk habitat. Note that this trail may be closed during times of high elk count.

Parking is adjacent to Deer Creek Canyon Road in a modified pullout. On summer afternoons, thunderstorms are a possibility.

Almost hidden among trees and brush, the string of this balloon loop begins on the Rattlesnake Gulch Trail. Look for a small sign identifying this multi-use trail. Dipping into a grassy drainage under cottonwoods and scrub oak, the path heads up an incline along a red soil traverse, escorted by wild plum thickets.

The gentle trail ascends on an east heading before plunging into a ravine. From here, it is a short lift to a nearly flat tableland of endless grass—perfect elk habitat. Traditionally, elk frequented the prime grazing areas of the High Plains. With man's expansion into the West, however, these

Trail Rating	easy
Trail Length	2.8-mile balloon loop
Elevation	5,950 to 6,200 feet
Amenities	none
Highlights	red-rock views
Location	South Valley Park, Jefferson County Open Space
Directions	From C-470 southwest of Denver, take the Wadsworth Boulevard exit and head south for 0.2 mile to South Deer Creek Canyon Road. Turn right and proceed for 3 miles to the pullout and parking area on the left. The trailhead is across the road.

animals were driven into the mountains. This grassy benchland adjacent to the foothills attracts elk in large numbers.

Red Fountain and buff Lyons Formations, with the Dakota Hogback behind, rise artistically from the east section of South Valley Park. The futuristic silver facade of Lockheed Martin's Deer Creek Facility lies to the northwest.

A right turn where the string of the balloon joins the loop sends hikers counterclockwise, the direction suggested in the park's brochure. Grasses dominate the landscape. Dropping gently into a small oak-shaded arroyo presents a change from the flats. A tiny stream, hidden by vegetation, comes as a surprise. The arroyo grows deeper downstream, starkly exposing red and white sandstone layers. Swinging around to the north, the trail keeps those red-rock views coming.

A connector trail veers right, while Grazing Elk Loop continues straight ahead. The red sandstone wall to the right of the silver building is reportedly the aerie of a pair of golden eagles.

The trail heads west through more grasses, including buffalo grass, on a slight incline. A causeway leads to willows and cattails, revealing the riparian influence of a hillside spring.

Curve around to meet ravines and a dry juniper-studded exposure. Views of Deer Creek Canyon Park unfold to the south. Soon the loop will complete its circuit and you will have only to retrace the short string to reach your vehicle.

For a satisfying cruising trail in the southwest suburban outskirts of metro Denver, Grazing Elk Loop in South Valley Park fits the bill.

Meadowlark/Plymouth Loop

Trail Rating	easy to moderate
Trail Length	2.7-mile loop
Elevation	6,100 to 6,550 feet
Amenities	restrooms, picnic shelters
Highlights	views, wildflowers
Location	Deer Creek Canyon Park, Jefferson County Open Space
Directions	From C-470 southwest of Denver, take the Wadsworth Boulevard exit, head south for 0.2 mile and turn right on Deer Creek Canyon Road. Follow this winding road, keeping your eyes out for Grizzly Drive on the left. Turn here, and proceed for 0.25 mile to the open space sign. The trailhead and parking area will be on your right.

Deer Creek Canyon Park, consisting of nearly 1,900 acres, is another star in Jefferson County's Open Space array. Conveniently close-in, it offers several trails through diverse habitats, including hiker-only 1.6-mile Meadowlark Trail. To complete the 2.7-mile loop, hikers join bikers on Plymouth Trail's lower 1.1 miles. The loop travels through open grasslands, scrub oak copses, stands of Douglas fir, and rocky riparian habitats. This land was once roamed by tribes of nomadic Indians including Ute and Arapaho, and, beginning in 1872, homesteaders staked their claims here.

Parking is in a large lot shared by hikers, bikers, horseback riders, and picnickers. Summer afternoons may brew up furious thunderstorms.

This route begins on the near side of the restrooms where crusher-fines line the trail, and passes picnic shelters with commanding views. Early summer presents a wide variety of wildflowers, such as tri-petaled spiderwort and cupped sego lily. This prime bloom-time applies to most of the foothills life zone. The path follows a shady ravine called Rattlesnake Gulch before switchbacking up the lower grassy slopes as they give way to shrubland.

Continue along an eastern exposure where interesting views of the Fountain Formation bring to mind the sculpted red sandstone found in Roxborough State Park and Garden of the Gods. Meadowlark Trail then levels through grasses and scrub oak before tracking along a south-facing slope for more of those great cityscape and plains views.

A few Douglas firs prepare the way as the trail drops into shade and joins Plymouth Creek Trail at a footbridge. Watch for butterflies such as tiger swallowtails and fritillaries here. Many species of butterflies are drawn to the lush vegetation found along Plymouth Creek as the trail descends beside it. It is interesting to note that Colorado boasts more butterfly species than any other state.

If you would rather not share your hike with mountain bikers, consider retracing hiker-only Meadowlark Trail. Choosing this bike free alternative adds 0.5 mile to your hike, for a total of 3.2 miles. Loop-minded hikers, turn left on Plymouth Trail to complete the described 2.7-mile circuit.

The road-wide track follows the stream and then curves into shrub-laced red sand. As the roadway turns back into a trail, meadow grasses that are interspersed with yucca join the last segment of the loop.

Deer Creek Canyon Park is just minutes off C-470, making it a fine spur-of-the-moment destination. While it can be hiked all year, the peak time to enjoy wildflowers here is spring and early summer. Meadowlark/Plymouth Loop is a convenient hike to add to this close-in collection.

Fountain Valley Loop

Trail Rating	easy
Trail Length	2.25-mile balloon loop (plus Lyons Overlook)
Elevation	6,100 to 6,250 feet
Amenities	visitor center, naturalist-led activities
Highlights	rock formations, views
Location	Roxborough State Park
Directions	From C-470 southwest of Denver, take the Wadsworth Boulevard exit and head south. Turn left on Waterton Road and continue for about 1.6 miles to Rampart Range Road. Turn right, proceed 2.3 miles to Roxborough Park Road, and turn left. The park entrance will be on the right. There is a fee to enter the park.

Abutting Pike National Forest, Roxborough State Park offers fine trails that travel through the transition life zone, hosting plant species of both the plains and the foothills. One of the most congenial routes is the Fountain Valley Loop. This balloon loop travels down a dry grassy valley to a historic stone house and returns through a lush valley flanked by fins of red sandstone. Options include two spur trails: One leads to an overlook highlighting the park's unique geology, and a second heads to an observation deck with a grand view. Before starting out, stop at the unique visitor center, which houses interactive displays and a bookstore.

Though the paved parking lots are usually adequate, fine-weather weekends sometimes find them full. Come early to avoid disappointment and, on summer days, the afternoon thunderstorms.

Leading north from the visitor center's flagstone patio, the roadway provides a surface geared for people of most hiking abilities. A low sign on the left admonishes: "Leaves of three, leave them be." Beware of poison ivy in the park.

Head along the graveled roadway, ascending slightly to a rise where the brief spur to Fountain Valley Overlook appears on the left. The spur ends at a pair of convenient back-to-back benches with breathtaking views. You can look west at 7,205-foot Carpenter Peak's granite top, northwest at the 300-million-year-old iron oxide-stained Fountain Formation, north to the buff-banded Lyons Formation, and east to the Dakota Hogback.

Back on the main trail, pass a large copse of scrub oak on the left that shelters a comfortable bench. The route forks here, and the trail on the right leads you counterclockwise on the loop.

Soon you'll approach a spur on the left for Lyons Overlook. Follow the signs to a spectacular view from the top of the petrified sand dunes of the Lyons Formation. As the trail levels at the top, pause at a bench or proceed to the overlook deck to view Roxborough State Park's splendid rock formations.

When heading back down, take the connector trail that angles left to return to the main roadway. Here, the route descends to the historic Persse Place. Built around 1900, the log outbuildings and stone house (which has since been restored) were owned by a man with high hopes of turning the Roxborough area into an upscale resort. The historic house is open for guided tours on occasion.

As the loop curves west, look over the trees at the distinctive rock formation. This area was once called Washington Park because of the likeness between the ridge's features and the profile of our nation's first President.

Passing Little Willow Creek, the trail travels into a wet meadow area bordered on the west by fins of soaring red sandstone. Pause at the frog signpost by the second creek crossing. In late April and May, the burbling of dime-size chorus frogs might be heard here.

Ahead and to the west, a grove of quaking aspens flourishes 1,300 feet below its typical elevation. The trail curves to pass The Sentinel, a towering finger of eroded red sandstone. Wind north past an oak-shaded bench as the rock-rimmed valley widens, just before the string of the balloon loop is reached. The visitor center signals the completion of the loop.

Just a brief drive from the Denver metro area, Roxborough State Park, a National Natural Landmark, is a rewarding getaway. The Fountain Valley Trail explores interesting aspects of this tranquil place.

Carpenter Peak

Roxborough State Park was a site where nomadic Indians gathered, leaving little evidence of their encampments aside from scattered artifacts and fire rings. Homesteaders including Julius Carpenter established claims here in the late 19th and early 20th centuries. Today the park is the realm of wildlife and day-use visitors who hike the diverse trails. The Carpenter Peak Trail is a good route to look for wildlife and a fine place to encounter seasonal wildflowers. The fabulous views are a bonus.

Parking in what appear to be adequate lots can fill on fine spring and summer weekends. Come early to secure a space and help avoid afternoon thunderstorms that typically roll in from the west.

Across from the unique visitor center, Carpenter Trail shares its beginning with Willow Creek Trail and heads immediately west into scrub oak. Along with wildflowers, poison ivy flanks the meandering path. Poison hemlock, a member of the parsley family that looks like Queen Anne's lace, spreads flat white umbels atop tall, hollow, purple-splotched stalks. Steer clear of these toxic plants. The trail narrows before an open area reveals the Lyons Formation, and beyond it, the Dakota Hogback.

A small footbridge leads through wickedly prickly hawthorn before the trail rises gently. Soon open sky and red soil show the way between mountain mahogany shrubs. Breaching scrub oak, Willow Creek Trail veers left, while the way to Carpenter Peak continues straight ahead. Come alongside a few aspens, growing far below their typical elevation, on the way to a clenched fist of red rock overlooking a little wildflower garden.

Trail Rating moderate

Trail Length 6.4-mile out-and-back

Elevation 6,100 to 7,200 feet

Amenities visitor center, interpretive displays, naturalist-led activities

Highlights soaring red sandstone formations, views, wildflowers

Location Roxborough State Park

Directions From C-470 southwest of Denver, take the Wadsworth Boulevard exit and head south. Turn left on Waterton Road and continue for about 1.6 miles to Rampart Range Road. Turn right, proceed 2.3 miles to Roxborough Park Road, and turn left. The park entrance will be on the right. There is a fee to enter the park.

In a sweeping hay meadow, another junction appears and South Rim Trail goes left, whereas Carpenter Peak Trail continues straight ahead. The route crosses a dirt road and is met by informative signs: One states that it is 2.6 miles to the peak, the other outlines safe behavior in mountain lion country. Wild plum thickets lead up to a shady ravine. Climb a short pitch where a brief social spur leads to a bench with a sensational view of the red Fountain Formation and beyond. Ascend to a curve for a north-facing wildflower display.

Switchbacks lift hikers to a glorious panorama of Roxborough's unique rock forms and the plains to the east. The trail then heads west to find a memorial bench resting in the cool shade of Douglas firs. Squared risers assist the next switchback, then a couple of rock steps bring you on up to a triple-trunked ponderosa pine and a ravine. Then the trail levels across a wildflower-spattered flat anchored by another restful bench. Dropping off the flat, the path curves around on an open slope and into Douglas fir shade again.

Traverse a southeast slope undulating toward a handy bench fronted by a well-crafted rock "patio." The stones here were set by Volunteers for Outdoor Colorado, an especially active group that constructed some of the Carpenter Peak Trail. VOC has worked on over 175 projects throughout the state.

The track pulls up into stunted oak where a sign announces that Carpenter Peak is 0.1 mile ahead to the right. Climb over rocky ground and steps on the last push to the summit. The top, a jumble of ancient granite boulders, makes a fine place to stretch your soul and enjoy views in every direction.

Close to the Denver metro area, Roxborough State Park is an intriguing destination. Its Carpenter Peak Trail offers superb vistas, colorful wildflowers, and captivating geologic formations as well as great exercise.

South Rim Loop

Trail Rating	easy to moderate
Trail Length	3-mile loop
Elevation	6,100 to 6,300 feet
Amenities	visitor center
Highlights	red-rock formations, views, naturalist-led activities, wildflowers
Location	Roxborough State Park
Directions	From C-470 southwest of Denver, take the Wadsworth Boulevard exit and head south. Turn left on Waterton Road and continue for about 1.6 miles to Rampart Range Road. Turn right, proceed 2.3 miles to Roxborough Park Road, and turn left. The park entrance will be on the right. There is a fee to enter the park.

Just southwest of metro Denver, Roxborough State Park's 3,400 acres are anchored by intriguing rock formations, including the sharp-ridged Dakota Hogback, the petrified sand dunes of the Lyons Formation, and the Fountain Formation's towering red fins. South Rim Trail can be accessed from the visitor center. Enter the unique center and peruse the interactive displays and information before striking out on this diverse loop.

Parking is in designated slots, which often fill on fine-weather weekends. Thunderstorms can form behind the Front Range foothills on warm summer afternoons.

Sharing a trailhead with Willow Creek Trail, South Rim Trail begins across the service road from the visitor center's patio. The path winds through abundant scrub oak and past poison-ivy patches. Look for airy bracken fern growing at the base of red sandstone on the right side of the trail.

Inviting benches beckon as the path leads to a small footbridge that leads through hawthorn. With wildflowers brightening the way, the trail heads up slightly, eventually coming to a junction. South Rim Trail goes straight ahead here, soon passing a disjunct copse of aspens. The next junction sends South Rim Trail to the left, within sight of a giant cottonwood sheltering another bench.

After crossing Little Willow Creek on a footbridge, ascend gently into thicker vegetation. The trail zigzags up to where Douglas firs offer shade.

Underfoot, the reddish decomposed sandstone path leads through a landscape of shrubs and rock formations.

A short spur on the right leads to one of many benches along South Rim Trail, this one sheltered by scrub oak. Enjoy its sweeping view to the east over rolling hills. Soon a railed overlook shows off Roxborough's northern rock collections: The Dakota Hogback is to the east, the middle is shared by the pale Lyons and the rusty red Fountain Formation, and Carpenter Peak's granite outcrops probe the western skyline. In the far distance, Denver's downtown skyline rises from the plains.

Following landform contours, the track switchbacks down to meet Willow Creek Trail again. At this juncture, a bench takes in a sweeping view of those signature rock formations. Wildflowers, such as mid-June-blooming sego lily, spatter the hillsides.

Continuing straight ahead along a dry, south-facing slope puts you on a descending slant where creeping grape holly thrives. In bloom-time, this hillside is a wealth of wildflowers. A sturdy railed bridge leads across a drainage, then the track bends to the west, paralleling the entrance road before crossing onto the north side and heading toward the parking lot.

Over five dozen wildflower species enhance the joy of a mid-June hike on the South Rim Trail. A grand collection of Roxborough State Park's impressive rock formations delights visitors year-round.

Willow Creek Loop

An excellent time to explore the trails of Roxborough State Park is early morning, when low-angled light bathes the rock formations in golden glow. This is also a good time for viewing wildlife such as mule deer. Close to the Denver metro area in miles, Roxborough State Park is worlds away in serenity. Visitors can gaze at towering fins of 300-million-year-old red sandstone. The unique visitor center features a collection of interactive exhibits and a fine selection of natural history books.

Parking is in paved lots that can fill completely on fine-weather weekends. For some solitude, try coming on a weekday morning. An early hike will also help you to avoid the thunderstorms that occur on summer afternoons.

West of the visitor center's patio, a sign directs hikers to 1.4-mile Willow Creek Trail, the shortest route in the park. Immediately entering scrub oak, the shaded path soon encounters a sign that warns of the prolific presence of poison ivy.

The sheltering scrub oak is also a favorite haunt of colonizing bracken fern, growing where sandstone outcrops collect moisture. As openings in the scrub oak appear, hikers can enjoy the views and look for wildflowers along the exposed edges of the track. The first opening is home to a wood bench that faces east toward the petrified sand dunes of the Lyons Formation.

Trail Rating	easy
Trail Length	1.4-mile loop
Elevation	6,100 to 6,000 feet
Amenities	visitor center, naturalist-led activities
Highlights	red-rock views, wildflowers
Location	Roxborough State Park
Directions	From C-470 southwest of Denver, take the Wadsworth Boulevard exit and head south. Turn left on Waterton Road and continue for about 1.6 miles to Rampart Range Road. Turn right, proceed 2.3 miles to Roxborough Park Road, and turn left. The park entrance will be on the right. There is a fee to enter the park.

Farther east, check out the Dakota Hogback's solidified mud layers laid down in the age of dinosaurs.

The level trail leads to a small footbridge and into spiny hawthorn harboring Canada violets. Wend up slightly to an area where early-blooming orchid penstemon flourishes in the lithic soil. The trail crunches underfoot as you approach a junction that is just shy of a few aspens determinedly growing 1,300 feet below their normal range.

Willow Creek Loop follows the left fork. The track drops gently through more scrub oak, reaching an open meadow on its way down to a child-sized footbridge spanning a tiny stream. Linger near the bridge to check out the horsetails and fresh-scented mint growing by the waterway. Directly ahead is a bench by a stand of willows flanking trickling Willow Creek.

If you're hiking Willow Creek Trail in mid to late May, look for birdfoot violet, a locally uncommon wildflower. After wandering through scrub oak, the trail emerges into the open, passing thickets of three-leaf sumac. Fiery orange Indian paintbrush pops up occasionally.

Soon you'll arrive at a junction with a bench, where the trail goes left and descends through bush and scrub oak woods. Pass yet another bench before the trail crosses a railed bridge. Continue straight ahead as the path parallels the entrance road and then crosses it on the way back to the parking lot. Well-sited benches appear along the way.

Roxborough State Park has been designated a National Natural Landmark and a Colorado Natural Area. Its scenic and short Willow Creek Trail makes for a good wildflower walk in spring and early summer.

Indian Creek

Trail Rating	easy
Trail Length	4-mile out-and-back
Elevation	7,480 to 6,800 feet
Amenities	restrooms
Highlights	peaceful woodland walk, wildflowers
Location	Pike National Forest
Directions	From C-470 southwest of Denver, exit at Santa Fe Drive (US 85) and head south. Turn right on Jarre Canyon Road (CO 67) and proceed 10.3 miles to the Indian Creek Campground on the right; the trailhead parking area is immediately to the left.

Looking for an easygoing shady wildflower jaunt accompanied by a clear stream? Indian Creek Trail, one of the few close-in accesses to Pike National Forest, fits the bill. Indian Creek Trail follows its namesake tributary through a lush ecosystem, descending gently to meet Bear Creek. From here, hikers who wish to extend their journey can set out on the Colorado Trail for a few miles.

Parking is plentiful, with lots of room for horse trailers. Conifer forest and riparian vegetation shade this hike, so approaching thunderstorms might be hidden from view. Be prepared for thunderstorm activity, particularly if you set out in the afternoon on a summer day.

Head west from the parking area down a wide gravel road to a meadow that hosts numerous wildflowers in spring. Off to the left, a hidden creek nourishes riparian species. Conifers shade the pathway down to an equestrian camping area, and the somewhat concealed trail veers off from a campsite at the far west end.

Dancing aspens flank the path down to a small rugged outcrop scabbed with lichen. Bennett Mountain's 8,045-foot bulk intercedes between the trail and the highway, and traffic noise is joyfully replaced by birdsong and the sound of running water. Descending, the track passes scrub oak and small aspen that shelter pristine meadow anemones and locally uncommon bird-foot violets in springtime.

Where the trees thin a bit, the narrowing track drops some, then levels under evergreens. Blue columbine, its spurred blossoms delicately redolent of honeysuckle, flourish here in mid-June. Aspen allow a bit of sky to filter through before denser woods return, and Indian Creek Trail undulates through alternating sun and shade.

The path switchbacks down to a double-log bridge spanning Bear Creek where alders and willows flank the waterway. The sky smiles on a grassy reach on the other side of the shallow creek as hikers continue north. The trail overlooks a stream bank where the waters tumble over worn stones.

Shaded again by forest, the leveling track enters scrub oak as the creek spills over small ledges of rock. The rough trail climbs up to a small pile of mine tailings. Look for a short tunnel on the left, almost obscured by overhanging vegetation, marking the turnaround place for the hike.

This trail eventually meets the marvelous Colorado Trail, and from there it is only some 450 sinuous, undulating, mountainous, backcountry miles to the route's western terminus outside of Durango.

Indian Creek Trail is a good bet for a quick creek-side trek through the woods. Not far from the Denver metro area, and just west of Sedalia, it offers a foray into wildflowers, birdsong, and a modicum of solitude.

Eastern Prairie

Picturesque and unexpected, the gash of Castlewood Canyon State Park beckons prairie travelers.

While hiking in Colorado is most often associated with alpine adventures, this region reveals what the east side of the greater Denver area offers for outdoor enthusiasts. Barr Lake State Park, in the metro area's northeastern reaches, is a mecca for birders and watchers of wetland wildlife. The Colorado Bird Observatory has established its headquarters here. At the south end of the region, Castlewood Canyon State Park is home to a precious section of the famous Black Forest, its once-grand stands of ponderosa pine virtually decimated by the "pineries" of the 1860s, which produced the lumber used to build much of early Denver and Colorado Springs. This park is split by a deep canyon, carved by Cherry Creek, in the midst of grassland.

In between, Cherry Creek State Park's lakeside trails and precious plots of Douglas County Open Space, including Glendale Farm and Columbine Parks, provide places for city-dwellers to seek solace. Let this region, and its convenient, close-in parks, surprise and delight you.

Contents

Eastern Prairie

Hikes 95 – 100

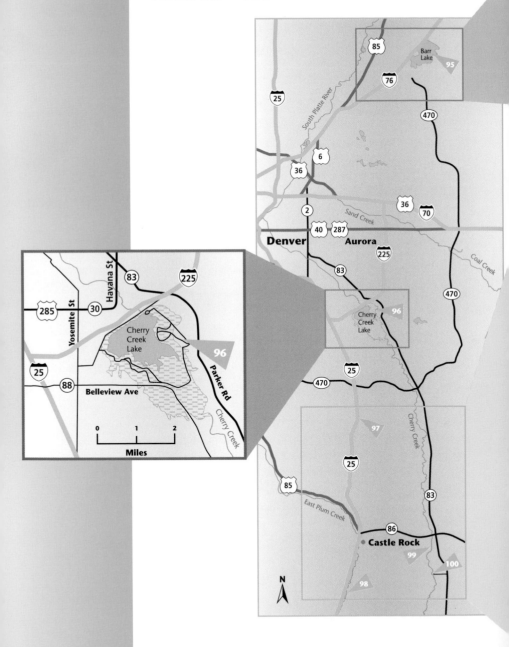

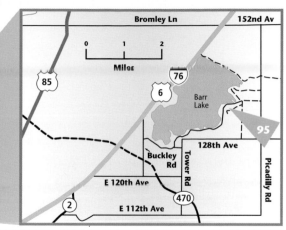

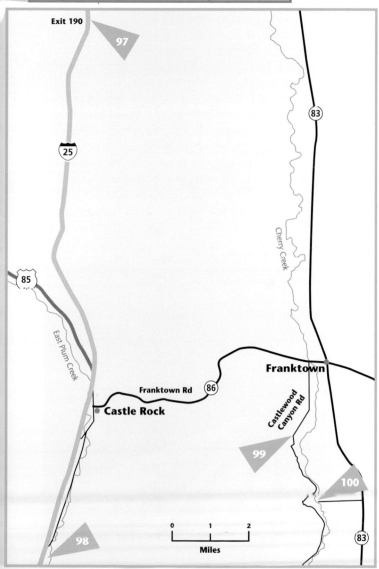

Hike 95

Gazebo Boardwalk/ Niedrach Nature Trail

Of the 2,700-plus acres that comprise Barr Lake State Park, over 1,900 of them are water. Barr Lake sits on the prairie southeast of Brighton, and is primarily used to store water for irrigation. Is also a great place to observe wildlife, especially some of the 330 avian species recorded at the park. Check with the visitor center for a bird list before heading out on the 1.3-mile trail to the Gazebo Boardwalk. Colorado Bird Observatory's research organization is headquartered at Barr Lake because of the area's abundant birdlife. In addition to monthly naturalist-led activities, an annual Fall Birding Festival is held here in late September. A boardwalk with an observation gazebo extends out over the lake.

The trail from the visitor center is flat and follows the perimeter of the lake out to the elevated boardwalk. For those desiring a longer hike, Barr Lake can be encircled in 8.8 miles. Parking is in large lots—one to the north, another to the south—shared by picnickers and other recreationists.

With a bird list from the visitor center in your hands, cross the bridge and turn left onto the trail. A sign says it is 1.3 miles to the Gazebo Boardwalk. Rustling overhead, cottonwoods accompany hikers on the right, while the Denver and Hudson Canal weaves on the left.

Trail Rating	easy
Trail Length	2.6-mile out-and-back (plus boardwalk)
Elevation	5,150 feet
Amenities	visitor center, picnic sites
Highlights	boardwalk, water birds, bald eagles
Location	Barr Lake State Park
Directions	From central Denver, take I-25 North to I-76 East. Turn right onto Bromley Lane and right onto Picadilly Road. The entrance to Barr Lake State Park is on the right. There is a fee to enter the park.

Soon the nifty Niedrach Nature Trail—part boardwalk, part observation deck—beckons on the right. Colorful interpretive signs inform visitors of wildlife residents, including hognose snakes, mule and white-tailed deer, and numerous bird species. Head right on a gravel path flanked by clumps of grass. Remount the boardwalk, elevated over wetlands, on your way to a covered observation deck.

Continue on the boardwalk to return to the main trail. A turn to the right takes the roadway past a bench or two. A short spur at the 1-mile mark accesses a wildlife observation station in the shadow of giant cottonwoods. A little detour through Fox Meadow leads visitors to another blind.

The trail serpentines over level ground, passing open shoreline wetlands before coming to a rail fence at the 1.3-mile point. A turn to the right carries hikers high above the lake on a boardwalk that doglegs among islands of willow. You'll see fine pale sand beneath the water's surface as you arrive at the final tree-anchored island that houses a gazebo. Commodious and sturdy, the octagonal structure sports benches around half its perimeter. From here, your eyes can skim the water for waterfowl and shorebirds. The west rail lines up with a silvery snag that casually points toward a bald eagle nest— the one for which Barr Lake has become famous. If you spot a big bird soaring effortlessly on flat outstretched wings, you might be observing a bald eagle.

The hike to Barr Lake State Park's Gazebo Boardwalk, with its brief stint on Niedrach Nature Trail, does indeed deserve a "wow!"

East Wetlands Loop

Cherry Creek State Park encompasses over 3,900 acres, including an 880-acre reservoir. This popular destination offers opportunities for nature study and a wide variety of recreational activities. The East Wetlands Preserve Loop weaves through a forest of cottonwood trees and feels far away from suburbia. It holds early morning treasures for bird- and other wildlife-watchers, and binoculars are encouraged. It's a good idea to pick up a map at the entrance station or park offices. No bikes or dogs are allowed in this preserve.

Parking is adequate; however, the whole park might fill to capacity on busy summer weekends. Come early to secure a spot at the trailhead and to avoid afternoon thunderstorms.

From the fence at the parking lot, turn left onto the East Wetlands Preserve Trail, which drops you onto a boardwalk. On the right, a minuscule pond, patched with diminutive duckweed floating like green confetti, hides among cattails and bulrushes. Continue to a colorful kiosk.

A gate welcomes you into a wildlife discovery zone as you head toward the level willow-walled string of the balloon loop. Look for raccoon tracks here—little handprints stamped in soft soil. The cottonwoods, alive with birds, grow so thickly that they form an almost continuous canopy. Bullocks orioles, western wood peewees, and goldfinches dart about, singing their unique songs. Ubiquitous cottontail rabbits freeze as if their immobile posture provides them with perfect camouflage. White-tailed deer, with their

Trail Rating	easy
Trail Length	1.2-mile balloon loop
Elevation	5,600 feet
Amenities	nearby restrooms
Highlights	bird-watching, shady stroll
Location	Cherry Creek State Park
Directions	From central Denver, take I-25 South to I-225, and head east to Parker Road (CO 83). Head south to Cherry Creek State Park's East Entrance Station on the right. Proceed 0.8 mile, turn left on East Lake View Road, and continue to the Shop Creek Trailhead on the right. There is a fee to enter the park.

spotted fawns in June and July, watch with chocolate-syrup eyes. This is a great trail to acquaint kids with nature, suburban-style.

After crossing a footbridge, you'll notice that the understory thickens. Prepare for an angled turn to the right. The wide path may introduce denizens such as yellow warblers, evening grosbeaks, and American robins.

An open meadow beckons and the trail winds around to a view of Cherry Creek Dam with Rocky Mountain National Park's resident four-teener, Longs Peak, in the distance. The path then turns south, narrowing as it reenters woods, and offers a glimpse of a cattail marsh on the right.

This next section, on singletrack trail, is a good place to watch for butterflies and dragonflies. An open grassy meadow leads to woods again. High willows flank the path, and golden currant provides fruit for the wide variety of birds that call this wetlands preserve home. A left turn brings you back down the path on which you came. The parking area is just ahead.

This level, tree-shaded balloon loop through Cherry Creek State Park's East Wetlands Preserve is an enjoyable outing for all ages. Bring binoculars if you wish to identify the birds whose songs add to the pleasure of your experience.

Glendale Farm Loop

Glendale Farm is a special respite in the busy corridor bisected by I-25. This loop, sited on a quarter section of rolling rangeland on Surrey Ridge, covers most of the 160 acres encompassed by the park. Strategically placed viewing benches and hitching rails make this new park a particularly user-friendly place to visit. Panoramic vistas to the west stretch from Pikes Peak in the south to Longs Peak in the north, and the space between is filled by Front Range mountains.

Parking in the fenced-in area is adequate and accommodates multi-use visitor vehicles. A caveat concerning the return to I-25 North: The merge lane sends you into fast-moving traffic. On summer afternoons, watch that mountain backdrop for developing thunderstorms.

The trail begins at the shaded southeast corner of the fenced parking area. Check out the Douglas County Parks rules and regulations sign at the green metal gate.

Pass over a shallow drainage and by an old remnant apple orchard. A turn to the right along a fence takes the trail south, parallel to I-25. A shallow drainage on the right deepens as the track wends up through some stands of scrub oak.

Trail Rating	easy
Trail Length	1.5-mile loop
Elevation	6,220 to 6,360 feet
Amenities	none
Highlights	mountain and prairie views
Location	Glendale Farm, Douglas County Open Space
Directions	From central Denver, take I-25 South to Exit 190. Go under I-25, proceed for 0.2 mile, and turn right onto a gravel entry road to access the fenced parking area.

Curving up through grasses, the route passes a log bench accompanied by a hitching rail. Rise on an S-curve to the well-defined arroyo, and proceed to a fence line that turns the winding path up to a ridge. The view opens to Pikes Peak to the south, Mount Evans front and center, and Longs Peak to the north—fourteeners, all three.

The high point of the loop is level, exposing wide sky and rolling range-land as far to the east as the eye can see. The land over which you look is prairie dog habitat. A log bench allows you to sit and contemplate the extent of the Great Plains and the march of Front Range mountains.

Cruise north through shortgrass prairie, featuring drought-tolerant buffalo grass. This spreading grass, named for its ability to rejuvenate after immense herds of bison grazed upon it, flanks the flat trail.

A fence line on the north boundary of Glendale Farm marks a spur that features excellent vistas, centered by 14,265-foot Mount Evans. Benches invite visitors to pause and take in the view. A variety of colorful rocks, once part of the conglomerate upon which they sit, now appear to be sprinkled on top. Though kids might be tempted to heft some of these ancient stones, it is against regulations to remove them. It's always better to let natural things lie so other people can enjoy them. Back on the main trail, wend down through scrub oak and grassland to finish the loop.

This 1.5-mile walk in Glendale Farm Open Space introduces you to a convenient section of rangeland with terrific views.

Columbine Loops

Trail Rating   easy

Trail Length   1.5-mile double loop

Elevation   6,000 feet

Amenities   picnic shelter, restrooms

Highlights   views of Pikes Peak

Location   Columbine, Douglas County Open Space

Directions   From Denver, take I-25 South to Castle Rock, Exit 182. Go south on the frontage road on the east side of the highway for 5 miles to the trailhead and parking area on the left.

Columbine's 170-plus acres include the North and South Loops, which combine to form a pleasant 1.5-mile hike. With its proximity to I-25, this bit of Douglas County Open Space is a convenient place to take a quick walk. Also part of the South I-25 Conservation Corridor Project, Columbine protects scenery, land, and wildlife including the Preble's meadow jumping mouse—a species listed as threatened by the U.S. Fish and Wildlife Service. The mouse's riparian habitat is closed to the public. Dogs are not permitted at Columbine Open Space.

In addition to the short double loop, a picnic shelter attracts visitors. Beyond the shelter an old barn and stone well-house bear witness to the thriving ranch that once sat on this land, formerly known as the Maytag property. Trains occasionally rumble through on tracks just east of the trail.

Shared by hikers, bikers, picnickers, and horseback riders, the parking area is generous for the size of the open space. The brief loops allow for a quick return if thunderstorms threaten on summer afternoons.

Begin the South Loop by heading right on a wide graveled route. Wildflowers dot the rangeland grasses. Ponderosa pine and scrub oak provide shelter for wildlife such as deer, coyote, elk, and smaller mammals. A knoll area on the right, back-dropped by towering pines, is topped by a pair of benches. The Preble's meadow jumping mouse habitat, watered by East Plum Creek and shaded by cottonwoods, lies below to the west.

The trail, flanked by a number of native grass species, drifts down to cross a sandy wash. When the route balloons, stay straight ahead and check out the distant view of 14,115-foot Pikes Peak.

Round the far end of the loop and circle quickly back if you choose. Alternately, you can take the approximately 0.5-mile extension spur for a longer hike. Access it by turning left to follow East Plum Creek's sandy flat floodplain south. A derelict barbed-wire fence signals the turnaround point if you have chosen the extra distance. Continuing on the original loop, briefly head west before curving around to the north, which brings you back to the parking area and the beginning of the second loop.

The North Loop starts out on the other side of the entrance road, and comes upon a sign that announces rattlesnake territory. On the left, an old beaver lodge can be seen as the wide track rises to a bench facing Pikes Peak. The balloon portion begins here.

A turn to the left leads the loop clockwise with views of buttes and lopped-off cones—the results of ancient volcanic activity. Smooth sumac, red-hued in autumn, fills a ravine in this grass-dominant landscape as the trail circles east. Pikes Peak draws attention in the distance as the loop finishes its balloon portion. Return to the parking area on the string segment.

Columbine Open Space calls you for a quick foray into ranchland.

Rim Rock Dam/
Creek Bottom Loop

Castlewood Canyon State Park features diverse landscapes and habitats as well as great picnic sites and scenic hikes. The East Entry, off CO 83, features a nice visitor center. The West Entry, from which the loop described here starts, accesses several unique trails. This 2,300-plus-acre park is anchored by ruins of a cut-stone dam built in 1890.

Parking is usually adequate at the trailhead. On summer afternoons, keep an eye out for approaching thunderstorms. Neither dogs nor horses are permitted on this trail.

From the parking area, head out on the Homestead Trail toward the ruins of a concrete structure where a posted map displays hiking trails. Wend down through scrub oak, passing sedimentary boulders and prickly pear cactus. Patches of poison ivy are also found on the way to a creek crossing, so be alert.

Turn left at an intersection onto Rim Rock Trail. Willows usher in a sturdy footbridge spanning Cherry Creek. Gambel oak, more commonly called scrub oak, accompanies the weaving track as it rises to a view of the canyon escarpment.

The path angles up through scrub, including mountain mahogany, as views of the famous Black Forest open to the north. Delicate pasqueflowers bloom here in early spring. Zigzag up to outcrops and curve around a north-facing exposure that supports Douglas fir.

Rock steps assist the next segment, until the last steep pitch lands you on top of rim-rock tableland. From here, elevation changes are minor and ponderosa pines create splashes of shade under otherwise open skies. Along this section, the route is sometimes bedrock and sometimes sand. Even when the trail fades, it quickly reappears, never straying far from the canyon's rim as it ventures south.

Views into Castlewood Canyon's evergreen depths may be complemented by the wobbling flight of turkey vultures. Far views of long-shouldered Pikes Peak probe the southern skyline. A bit farther, a canyon edge reveals the eroded depths of Cherry Creek's palely bedded drainage. Much of the carving was done in just one day when the dam upstream broke in 1933 and caused a disastrous flood.

As you contour Castlewood's brink, note the prairie grasses and several kinds of cacti clinging to the shallow-soiled rim rock. Seeps create damper pockets that host interesting plants as well.

Descend into Castlewood Canyon where Rim Rock Trail appears to vanish. The initial drop is the most tricky as it makes an oblique turn to the right. From here, the trail switchbacks down to a junction where the loop angles right. Look for stairs that take you to the remains of the old cut-stone dam. Span the creek on a footbridge, then stay close to the stream, heading right again to travel on willow-flanked Creek Bottom Trail.

As you dip below the canyon rim, sporadic boulders guide you to an unexpected copse of quaking aspen. You'll come to a rail fence guarding an overlook of the creek's small falls. On the near side of the road, head up steps and undulate through a long stretch of forest and oak, at last rejoining Homestead Trail for the return to your vehicle.

The Rim Rock Dam/Creek Bottom Loop offers interesting geology, history, diverse habitats, and plenty of spots to enjoy the views.

Trail Rating	easy to moderate
Trail Length	4.2-mile loop
Elevation	6,280 to 6,100 to 6,500 feet
Amenities	restrooms, picnic sites
Highlights	dam ruins, creek, rim-rock canyon
Location	Castlewood Canyon State Park
Directions	From Denver, take I-25 South to Castle Rock and head east on Franktown Road (CO 86). Proceed to Castlewood Canyon Road, turn right, and continue roughly 2 miles to the park entrance station. The trailhead is 0.1 mile on the left. There is a fee to enter the park.

Lake Gulch/Inner Canyon Loop

Trail Rating	easy
Trail Length	2-mile loop
Elevation	6,600 to 6,400 feet
Amenities	picnic sites, visitor center, restrooms
Highlights	views, prairie, creek canyon, naturalist-led activities
Location	Castlewood Canyon State Park
Directions	From Denver, take I-25 South to Castle Rock and head east on CO 86 for 6 miles to Franktown. Turn right onto CO 83 (South Parker Road) and continue for 5 miles to the park's east entrance on the right. There is a fee to enter the park.

Eastern Douglas County offers an unexpected surprise in the midst of the rolling plains that dominate the region. Castlewood Canyon, with its distinctive Black Forest and deep canyon, is a prairie anomaly. The state park itself contains diverse habitats, from sunny riparian and deep-shaded Douglas fir to scrub oak and shallow-soiled rocky shelves. A welcoming visitor center has a labeled native plant garden, an informative slide show, and a helpful staff. Park maps are also available here.

A hike on Lake Gulch/Inner Canyon Loop is a perfect excursion for adventurous kids. The promise of a playful sandy-bottomed creek is all the incentive they need on a warm summer's day. Parking, shared by picnickers, is usually adequate. Watch for developing summer afternoon thunderstorms.

Lake Gulch Trail begins at the northernmost parking lot. The wide path is accompanied by wildflowers as it heads northwest, past picnic shelters and into open grasslands.

As the trail starts down, skirting shelves of rock and stunted scrub oak, ponderosa pine boughs provide pools of cool shade. Several types of rock appear along the trail including pastel rhyolite, composed of compressed volcanic ash; pale Castlewood Canyon Conglomerate, looking like a child's collection of pebbles embedded in crude concrete; and worn sheets of layered sandstone, featured at the far end of the loop.

The track narrows as it descends into Lake Gulch—once a reservoir fed by Cherry Creek. As the footpath curves down, pause to look south toward open valley ranchland that was exposed when the Cherry Creek Dam broke in 1933. Flooding their disastrous way clear to downtown Denver, the pent-up waters took two lives and did 1-million-dollar's worth of damage. Today's gurgling stream hardly resembles the raging torrent set loose when the dam, built in 1890, finally succumbed to the water's whim. Waves of smooth brome grass, a wildly invasive nonnative, surround the path as it approaches the remains of the old stone dam.

After crossing a footbridge over West Cherry Creek, Inner Canyon Trail leads the loop to the right. The creek flows alongside, caressing huge boulders amidst pockets of rough sand. Some sizable slabs by the creek are perfect places for a pause, a snack, or a snooze. The trail undulates through these hefty rocks before advancing more levelly in the shade of evergreen and oak. Poison ivy is at home here, and, in some places, advances close to the path.

The trail crosses Cherry Creek again before rising quickly on a series of steps for a steep but brief segment. Emerging through shrubs at the canyon's rim, continue forward to find a concrete walk that leads to the loop's end. Along this short leg back to the parking area, you can reacquaint yourself with appealing prairie wildflowers.

Castlewood Canyon State Park is a great destination that offers year-round recreation. Varied habitats, especially those along the creek, make for an interesting hike.

Appendix
Land Management Contacts

USDA Forest Service
www.fs.fed.us

**Arapaho & Roosevelt
National Forests**
Boulder Ranger District
2140 Yarmouth Avenue
Boulder, CO 80301
(303) 541-2500

Clear Creek Ranger District
101 Chicago Creek Road
Idaho Springs, CO 80452
(303) 576-3000

Pike National Forest
South Platte Ranger District
19316 Goddard Ranch Court
Morrison, CO 80465
(303) 275-5610

Colorado Division of Wildlife
6060 Broadway
Denver, CO 80216
(303) 297-1192
www.wildlife.state.co.us

Colorado State Parks
www.parks.state.co.us

Barr Lake
(303) 973-3959

Castlewood Canyon
(303) 688-5242

Chatfield
(303) 791-7275

Cherry Creek
(303) 699-3860

Eldorado Canyon
(303) 494-3943

Golden Gate Canyon
(303) 582-3707

Roxborough
(303) 973-3959

County Parks & Open Space

**Boulder County
Parks & Open Space**
2045 13th Street
Boulder, CO 80302
(303) 441-3950
www.co.boulder.co.us/openspace

**Douglas County
Division of Open Space
& Natural Resources**
100 Third Street
Castle Rock, CO 80104
(303) 660-7495
www.douglas.co.us/dc/recreation

**Jefferson County
Parks & Open Space**
700 Jefferson County Parkway
Suite 100
Golden, CO 80401
(303) 271-5925
www.co.jefferson.co.us

City Parks & Open Space

**City of Boulder
Open Space & Mountain Parks**
66 South Cherryvale Road
Boulder, CO 80303
(303) 441-3440
www.ci.boulder.co.us/openspace

**City and County of Denver
Department of Parks & Recreation**
Mountain Parks District
P.O. Box 1007
Morrison, CO 80465
(303) 697-4545
www.denvergov.org

Index

About the Author & Photographer

Author Pamela Irwin has been a volunteer naturalist at Roxborough State Park since the early 1980s. Her extensive background in and love of wildflower identification has earned her the certified title of Native Plant Master from Colorado State University. Pamela is also a member of the Rocky Mountain Nature Association, the Rocky Mountain Chapter of the American Rock Garden Society, Windflowers Garden Club, and the Audubon Society.

Photographer David Irwin purchased his first 35mm SLR camera as a teenager and has been behind a lens ever since. His favorite subjects include people of foreign lands, the remnants of past civilizations, and the textures of western terrain.

Avid hikers, Pamela and David enjoy combining their talents to produce beautiful hiking guidebooks to their home state. Previous collaborations include *Colorado's Best Wildflower Hikes Volume 1: The Front Range* and *Colorado's Best Wildflower Hikes Volume 2: The High Country*. They also

maintain an extensive slide library and have given slide-illustrated talks for various organizations including the Colorado Mountain Club. Additionally, many of David's photographs and Pamela's watercolors are now in private collections.